BEING
RELIGIOUS
IN
AMERICA

BEING RELIGIOUS IN AMERICA

The Deepening Crises over Public Faith

ERLING JORSTAD

AUGSBURG Publishing House • Minneapolis

BEING RELIGIOUS IN AMERICA
The Deepening Crises over Public Faith

Library of Congress Cataloging-in-Publication Data

Jorstad, Erling, 1930–
  BEING RELIGIOUS IN AMERICA.

  Bibliography: p.
  1. United States—Religion—1945–   2. United
States—Religious life and customs.   I. Title.
BL2525.J67   1986   291.1'7'0973   86-3360
ISBN 0-8066-2222-9

Manufactured in the U.S.A.   APH 10-0585

1   2   3   4   5   6   7   8   9   0   1   2   3   4   5   6   7   8   9

To Oscar and Connie
Curtis and Frieda
Elsie and Lloyd
and the memories of Doris and Harley—
all of whom were blessings as
brothers and sisters to
the baby of the family

Contents

Acknowledgments

Thanks to St. Olaf College for two Faculty Development Fund grants, and to a number of friends who constitute a valuable clipping service: my brother Curtis, my son Eric, Harlan Foss, Janet Gilbert, Michael Leming, Susan Lindley, Charles Lutz, Karen Petersen, Jim Tallon, and Emily and James White. Thanks to my typist, Lois Wilkens, who again typed a manuscript of mine with her customary intelligence and good humor.

CHAPTER ONE

Being Religious in America: What Is at Stake?

A leader in the American Jewish community celebrated the religious freedom of this nation with a verbal rhapsody:

Our America: a land where religious groups proliferate. It is a country of a variety of churches, faiths, and creeds, each enjoying full religious autonomy, guaranteed by the Constitution, and each reflecting a culture inspired by many men and women in their search for the meaning of life and the purpose of existence.

Our America: a land of churches in which people talk to God in many languages, pray to a deity in unique, mysterious, and sometimes in highly emotional and charismatic ways; where they follow practices and traditions dating to ancient times, yet couched in modern dress; where houses of worship are found everywhere, ranging from cellars, barns, and storefront rooms to pretentious and magnificent edifices. . . .

Our America: where the church is more than just a place for worship; where it operates day-care agencies for children, promotes scouting and numerous other club activities; where it engages in sports, recreation, and dramatics; where it offers guidance and counsel in matters of marriage, divorce, delinquency, alcoholism, and drug addiction; where psychologists and psychiatrists are on the ministerial staff; and where "Dial-a-Prayer" telephone service is available on a 24-hour basis. . . .

Our America: where highways and byways display billboards, large and small, with exhortations for personal salvation; where automobiles display theological decals on bumpers and rear windows with such typical slogans as "Smile, God Loves You," and "Christ Is Peace," and "Honk, If You Love Jesus.". . .

Our America: where ecumenism has reached high levels, with Christians and non-Christians worshiping together on special occasions; ministers, priests, and rabbis exchange pulpits; where clergy associations composed of Catholics, Greek Orthodox, Protestant, and Jewish spiritual leaders meet regularly to engage in dialogue; where blacks are nominated and elected to high office in large religious denominations.[1]

But a battle-scarred Roman Catholic priest sees another religious America:

Does America exist? Which America? The America that spent $2.5 trillion on war and war preparations in the last forty years? The America of 26,000 nuclear warheads; the America of the first-strike policy (or diplomacy)? The America that intervenes illegally in El Salvador, Lebanon, Nicaragua, Grenada; the America that manipulates Israel as a proxy, an accomplice, and a victim in the Middle East, in Africa, and in Central America; the America that spies on its citizens, eroding civil liberties, the America of 1984, where war is peace, falsehood is truth, lawlessness is law, rebellion is Marxism, rearmament is defense, and the MX is a "peacekeeper?" Of course, *that* America exists: Western Europeans and Third Worlders know its blindness, waste, and truculence better than most of us in this country.

Yet that spokesman, Philip Berrigan, can still celebrate religious freedom:

> So much for one America; now to the other. Fortunately for all of us, it, too, exists, a testimony against the first and an indictment of it. Unlike the Brahmins of the first, its members—having been freed by deprivation, passionate truth, outrage at injustice, sacrifice, persecution, imprisonment, and risk of death—considered egoism, ambition, and greed as inhuman. It is the America of John Woolman, Sojourner Truth, Lucy Stone, William Lloyd Garrison, W.E.B. Du Bois, Mother Mary Jones, Harriet Tubman, Bill Haywood, Eugene Debs, Fiorello La Guardia, Thomas Merton, Martin Luther King Jr., Dorothy Day, and thousands of others.
>
> This "cloud of witnesses" redeemed their times by giving the victims a voice, hands, and a defense against the slave masters, warmongers, robber barons, ideologues, venal politicians and judges. My brother Dan, a poet and member of this illustrious minority, calls these witnesses "mystics with hands."[2]

Besides these, still other Americans today show us how they express their faith in public. Having been silent for years over our current crises, they in a variety of ways are being religious in America. Some chain themselves to a fundamentalist day school in Nebraska, protesting alleged state interference. Some pastors engage in civil disobedience, risking the loss of their ordination to protest systemic poverty among mill workers. Some, ranging in age from teens to the eighties, march and accept arrest in front of munitions plants. Some protect unregistered aliens within the sanctuary of their churches. Some lobby in legislative halls for new public policies. They, too—like the rabbi and the priest—seek to be religious in America.

In the United States we celebrate our religious freedom, we make use of our liberty to dispute over it with our neighbors, and we make sure everyone knows we want *more* religious commitment to energize our public lives.

At the same time we believe our faith is a private matter. Each of us holds strong private convictions about how private faith should influence our public behavior, and we get upset when someone else tells us our particular faith is less than adequate for being truly religious in this country. The recipe each of us has for the best possible blending of religion and politics is not one that any of us is eager to change.

Yet today we also sense that we can no longer simply ignore the insistent demands of those who are going public with their faith, because too much is at stake. Just what is at stake? That is the subject of this book.

As religion has gone public, it has created deepening hostility and partisanship among us. We are being "tribalized" to an extent unknown before in our history. Each "tribe" sees its own religious commitments as the standard by which to exclude those outside its boundaries. Hence we discover conflict between "liberal" and "conservative," between "feminist" and "chauvinist," between "sectarian" and "secularist," between "nationalist" and "one worlder," between "libertarian" and "collectivist," between "elitist" and "rank and file," to name some among many divisions. We wonder why after more than 200 years of pursuing religious freedom as a people, we find ourselves involved in more conflict, more contention, more public acrimony over what being religious in America means.

The Issues that Divide Us

This book speaks to that concern. We explore in Chapter 2 how and why such a situation has occurred. In Chapters 3 through 6 we explore four crises: (1) patriotism, (2) pluralism and the new religions, (3) religion and politics, and (4) public-school education. This list is selective, not only because of limitations of space but because any such list would vary among us; hence, this list is offered as representative, not exhaustive.

These four controversies are public issues: they focus on our lives in society rather than on our interior, spiritual ways of being religious. This choice should not be interpreted to mean that I minimize the importance of the inner life. My choice rather is a recognition of the evergrowing realization that our faith leads us into the "public square" (as Richard John Neuhaus calls it).

Is being religious in America significantly different from being religious somewhere else? The religious impulse, certainly, is universal, known to all peoples in all places. But each of us lives in a particular place at a particular time. We all are subject to the laws, customs, and traditions of our place of residence, and these vary from nation to nation. Furthermore, many people believe that being a member of their country does mean that their religious expression is unique and, in some cases, superior to others. Recognizing this, I focus on the United States.

What that focus shows is that Americans are becoming more contentious and divided over public faith. Whatever informal consensus existed since 1776 over being religious in society has in the last two decades or so been severely challenged; some observers think that the consensus has, in fact, been destroyed.

Today questions that have always been raised in the past are being raised again with a new, more urgent fervor: Whose country is it anyway? Who is in control? Is it the majority of voters with their elected representatives? Is it the judges in the courts? Is it some loud and aggressive minorities (ethnic, gender, ideological) whose agenda breaks sharply with that of the majority? Is it the sectarians or the secularists, the Moral Majority, or the American Civil Liberties Union? Americans are doing battle in the pulpits, in the media, in the public schools, in the legislatures, and in the courts in an attempt to protect and advance their own expressions of what being religious in America means.

A further complication emerges from our inability to agree with one another over what religion is all about. Is it theological doctrine? Is it our moral lives in society? Is it the personal experience we feel but cannot fully define? Is it, in essence, a matter of knowledge—the information we have about the basic commonalities of faith around the globe?

This book is offered as one place to start reaching agreement. It has three features especially designed for that purpose. Each chapter concludes with a "What Is at Stake?" section. Here the issue is summarized, and the reader has the opportunity to reflect on what that issue means directly in his or her life. Second, each chapter has a set of discussion questions at its conclusion to help initiate the sharing of insights, examples, criticisms, and solutions for the issues at stake. Finally, Chapter 7 is my own attempt at spelling out, with specific examples, the ways in which we can be religious in America. Call them guidelines, or pointers, or insights—they are offered as a way towards understanding. There is also a bibliography of selected readings for further exploration of these themes.

I would be delighted to hear from any readers who are inclined to write their reactions. I promise to answer as quickly as possible.

Discussion Questions

1. What do you see as issues that divide Americans into "tribes"?
2. Why does religious faith divide us? Is all such division unhealthy?
3. How can religious faith unite or reconcile us?
4. Are there signs this is happening?

CHAPTER TWO

Strange and Troubled Times: Public Faith in America Since 1945

The words of two futurists help us understand our past, how we worked our way into the deepening crisis. John Naisbitt of *Megatrends* advises us, "The most reliable way to anticipate the future is by understanding the present."[1] That "present" is outlined for us by Alvin Toffler:

> A new civilization is emerging in our lives, and blind men everywhere are trying to suppress it. This new civilization brings with it new family styles; changed ways of working, loving, and living; a new economy; new political conflicts; and beyond all this an altered consciousness as well. Pieces of this new civilization exist today. Millions are already attuning their lives to the rhythms of tomorrow. Others, terrified of the future, are engaged in a desperate, futile flight into the past and are trying to restore the dying world that gave them birth.
>
> The dawn of this new civilization is the single most explosive fact of our lifetimes.[2]

From the vantage point of the mid-1980s that civilization first appeared clearly on the radar screen
of history around 1945. Since then American life has
undergone more fundamental changes than in any
previous era.

1945–1960

The end of World War II stands out as a moment
in which humankind witnessed the appearance of a
new age. As hostilities ceased, ending one era, a new
series of crises demanded immediate attention. The
most pressing of these included attending to the basic needs of life for the millions of refugees displaced
during the war. The world also had to come to terms
somehow with the enormity of the Nazi crime of ex-
terminating some six million Jews and others. Alongside that was the chilling horror that since detonat-
ing the atomic bombs over Japan, humankind could
now destroy all life on this planet. Finally, the hopes
for world peace quickly vanished before the armed
conflict between the Soviet Union and the United
States for strategic global dominance. These were no
times for faint hearts.

As the postwar years unfolded, the enormity of
these changes called forth what seemed an appropriate response from people of faith in America. A
religious revival, or at least a strong resurgence of
interest in religion emerged across the country. As
though to counter the perceived Soviet threat to
American values, church people sought to strengthen
the traditional American commitments to representative government, a free market, private property, and patriotism. These values, leaders taught,

surely had been the will of God for this nation; these values certainly would help repel the spiritual imperialism of antireligious communism.

Evidence of this new quickening turned up in several areas. One was the growing popularity of the old-fashioned revivalism of Billy Graham, a dynamic spokesman for traditional values. Some Americans found comfort in reaffirming traditional expressions of individualistic self-help, this time known as "positive thinking." Still others sought solace through several variations of the "Peace with God" motif of faith.

The statistics served to underline the trend. Americans joined churches and synagogues in increasing numbers; they financed an impressive number of church buildings; they contributed a record high in weekly pledges; attendance at Sabbath and Sunday services rose and remained high. Enrollments in church colleges, in college religion courses, and in seminaries grew rapidly. Public expression and involvement suggested that Americans were increasing their long-standing conviction that religion was helpful to the needs of the seeker and to the nation on which God had smiled.

Yet at the same time some blunt facts pointed to the distance the United States had yet to go in fulfilling its dreams. Its people had failed to come to terms with agonizing moral dilemmas such as racial discrimination, suppression of political dissent, continued subordination of women and ethnic minorities, rampant materialism, and exploitation of natural resources. How could we claim God's special providence on us and still allow such evils? The answer came back quickly. Despite its flaws, the United States was indeed God's special experiment. Who could doubt this as the United States contained Soviet expansion, created the world's highest standard of living, provided the greatest opportunity in all history for getting an education, and protected religious liberty. That was evidence of our solidarity with God.

Historians saw the 1950s as the age of "consensus." The United States had become great because its people really at heart agreed on key values more than they were divided over the moral dilemmas. The churches, with some notable exceptions, either endorsed the consensus position or pursued the privatized, individualist expression of faith. To most, being religious in America meant endorsing the national government's resistance to communism, supporting traditional economic values, being busy in local parish life, and advocating a gradual approach toward correcting the injustices of social life.

The 1960s

In the 1960s the understanding and expression of being religious in America underwent an astounding transformation. With little advance notice an awakening of monumental proportions broke out, involving its most fundamental institutions and ideals. The speed of that awakening, the events of the decade, and the intensity of the feelings generated combined to challenge the very meaning of being religious. Before the decade passed, Americans became at the same time both more antagonistic toward each other and more hopeful than in the 1950s about the future. They were divided because the proponents for reform demanded an end to the comfortable status quo of the 1950s and used confrontational agitation rather than consensus building as their mode of reform. Yet hope flourished all the while because for many participants America stood on the brink of fulfilling its promise of liberty for all and peace for a battered world.

Turmoil abounded throughout the period, because the movement for reform was so many-sided, even including contradictory goals. Well could one critic ask, "What could one say about the sixties that would be wrong?"[3] We watched the rise and fall of hippies and flower power; Selma and Watts; "God Is Dead" and "God Bless You Real Good"; black, brown, grey, gay power; pro-life and pro-choice; the ages of Aquarius and Narcissus; theologies of play, hope, liberation, process, secularity, and story; and key words like *relevance* and *roots*. Paradox abounded, and was celebrated by many as proof that being religious was taking on new life-transforming powers for those willing to risk.

Obviously such energy drew on long-standing and deep sources of nourishment; the age did not just blossom forth out of thin soil. During the previous decade the consensus view of approval for America failed to persuade the soon-to-be-dissenters. Their day now came as they built support, and established new tactics and goals.

The key word for the dissenters was *liberation*— from racial injustices, from sexual stereotypes, from a prevention of a full realization of every person's potential to contribute to society, and from reliance on military force to keep a Pax Americana around the globe. For those caught up in liberation, to be religious meant to find one's way in association with like-minded fellow seekers in new sisterhoods, brotherhoods, fellowships, tribes, and clans. All this occurred in the name of religion based on universal moral truths. Being religious meant getting directly involved in the dilemmas of American life. Because this nation claimed to be founded on the truths of life, liberty, and the pursuit of happiness, now was the time to make them happen.

This new vision created a major dilemma for the churches. As custodians and proclaimers of certain universal truths, they understood the need to speak out on social issues, such as those the liberationists were raising. The clergy could hardly avoid taking positions on the moral issues. Yet when some did speak out for one or more liberationist causes, they inevitably met sharp opposition from fellow clergy and laity. The dilemma became clear: to make a stand on highly controversial issues was being faithful to what these clergy believed, but by so doing they risked alienating other church people and losing the capacity to serve as mediators among discordant groups.

What was at stake? The talk about brotherhood and sisterhood meant supporting the controversial legislation for civil rights. The talk about peace and good will meant calling on the American government to end its military role in Southeast Asia. The talk about environmental issues meant calling on American capitalism to change its priorities. The talk about women's rights meant the creation of a radically different equalitarian society.

Voices for reform were challenged by voices for the status quo. Members insisted that the churches should concentrate on traditional, person-centered issues and avoid the bitter rancor produced by the liberationist agendas. That response, however, only encouraged the reformers to carry forward their battles.

Throughout this period some careful observers detected the beginnings of the end of a distinct, unified 400-year period of American religious life (the estimate of Sydney Ahlstrom).[4] Another watcher, William McLoughlin, suggested the 1960s were more than an age of revival. In essence they constituted an awakening, the latest of several historical "periods of cultural revitalization that begin in a general crisis of beliefs and values and extend over a period of a generation or so, during which time a profound reorientation in beliefs and values take place. Revivals alter the lives of individuals; awakenings alter the world view of a whole people or culture."[5] Awakenings, he wrote, break out in periods of cultural disorientation and grave personal stress, when citizens have lost faith in the legitimacy of their norms, the soundness of their institutions, and the capacity of the leaders of church and state to govern.

In the 1960s America underwent such a fundamental shift in its religious and moral expression. Some observers wondered even if God had died. Others predicted the demise of the local parish. Roman Catholics were trying to cope with earthquake-size controversies over doctrine, liturgy, and polity.

Some understood the shift as a matter of gaps: gaps between generations, between social classes, between females and males, between whites and people of color, between hawks and doves, between developers and protectors of natural resources, between activists and standpatters. The presence of such gaps indicated that for many the nature of what it meant to be religious had changed profoundly. The older consensus and expectations no longer prevailed.

Some became involved in "underground churches," meeting outside the sanctuaries, celebrating with coffee and doughnut Eucharists as one example of the new eclectic spirit. Worship services were turned into "celebrations," where ministers wore paisley vestments, handed out balloons or daisies, and encouraged dancing in the aisles. Jazz masses flourished under the name of "alternative liturgies"; guitars and recorders replaced pipe organs.

Some chose to avoid churches altogether, and yet considered themselves religious. In 1969 Thomas Luckmann termed this trend as *invisible religion*. By choice, he stated, seekers were keeping their faith private, free from institutions watching over them. This faith was consciously eclectic, drawing from whatever the participant found "relevant" in natural science, religions, experiences of one's youth.

The participants found all this to be liberating, relevant, and "now." Those who chose to stand outside of its boundaries found it a hodgepodge, a mishmash, a rejection of permanent truths. The thoughtful observers found this trend to be an expression of privatization—choosing greater individual expression in teaching and expression. Emerging directly out of the liberationist agendas, this privatization showed indifference, rather than hostility, toward the institutional church. It glorified personal choice and freedom, and it celebrated diversity. Fulfillment, being in tune with that which was infinite and ultimate, was now a matter of individual choice.

Yet beneath this apparent anarchy of invisible/individual religion stood a firm, unifying theme frequently expressed as "All you need is love." All one needed was to accept the goal of personal growth, become sensitive to the needs of others, get in touch with one's own feelings, tune in on the spiritual vibrations, find the religious life within one's own impulses celebrating wholeness, and be fully human and sincere. For some, to be religious meant to celebrate what was truly human. And what was the best quality of being human but that of love?

But how could a seeker know concretely what love meant? How could she or he avoid the criticism from traditionalists that this was little more than sentimental hokum dressed up with human-potential, therapeutic jargon? Didn't this prove that pop psychology had replaced the values and commitments of the organized communities of faith?

The answers to such charges emerged not from one or even a few spokespersons, nor from a single organization, but from an informal but widely agreed on loyalty to a system of ideas known as *expressive ethics*. A brilliant definition is that of Richard Sennett:

> The reigning belief today is that closeness between persons is a moral good. The reigning aspiration today

is to develop individual personality through experiences of closeness and warmth with others. The reigning myth today is that the evils of society can all be understood as evils of impersonality, alienation, and coldness. The sum of these three is an ideology of intimacy: social relationships of all kinds are real, believable, and authentic the closer they approach the inner psychological concerns of each person. This ideology transmutes political categories into psychological categories. This ideology of intimacy defines the humanitarian spirit of a society without gods; warmth is our god.[6]

With this, many seekers discovered a road to travel (if not a destination), one that offered none of the familiar ties to kinship, religious fellowship, or civil friendship, which had not provided them adequate psychic support. Unable to trust the traditional teachings of such stabilizing institutions as church, state, or school (which they saw as permeated by racism, sexism, etc.), they found instead self-actualization—that is to say, themselves. Or so the language of the day instructed them. Closeness and warmth helped "liberate individuals by helping them get in touch with their own wants and interests, freed from the artificial constraints of social rules, the guilt-inducing demands of parents and other authorities and the fake promises of illusory ideals such as love."[7] Neither money, nor work, nor social status could replace the new center of the self, the expression and experience of feelings. Discovering that, through the process the experts called "expressive ethics," the new believers could get close to others, and in so doing, realize their full humanity. This was a new way of being religious.

Today such terminology and such optimism may seem quaint, yet for those Americans who had failed to find rapport with the-way-religion-had-always-been, expressive ethics offered a viable alternative. The seeker could not halt the war in Vietnam, nor produce equal civil rights for every citizen, nor eliminate sexism or environmental pollution. But one could redesign one's inner, private life to be open to what was the most loving and human. Who could tell where that commitment might lead?

The 1970s

Just as the liberationists and the expressivists of the 1960s had demanded church support for their agendas, so the standpatters of the 1970s would demand that the churches endorse *their* particular priorities. America would, as observers began to notice, start to fragment, to "Balkanize" into smaller special interest groups, to retribalize around what people considered nonnegotiable in their religious understanding. This decade too would be strange and troubled, dominated by several diffuse trends: a decline of the mainline churches, increasing interest in Asian and heavily experiential religions, a marked surge of growth in fundamentalist and evangelical denominations, something close to a traditional revival, and, as a fitting finale to so odd an era, the emergence of high-powered political activism among Christians never before involved in that arena. Being religious in America was still what each seeker chose it to be.

In a decade of surprises, none was greater than the first noticeable trend—a substantial decline in membership, financial contributions, and public leadership in the mainline denominations. At the forefront of the civil rights, peace, and women's movements during the 1960s, mainline leaders now discovered they had failed to persuade large numbers of laity to join their crusades. National polls showed that the rank and file in the churches continued to express strongly negative attitudes towards the new social activism, and to reject the leaders' priorities for social-action programs. This trend first emerged in the late 1960s. By the mid-1970s losses of 10 percent or more were being reported by the Episcopalians, Presbyterians, United Methodists, and the United Church of Christ. Parallel to that was a clear decline in weekly attendance and support for outreach programs.

Among the several explanations of this decline, perhaps the most convincing is that the potential new members, those in their 20s and 30s, were staying away. They had in their own ways gone over to the "invisible religion" of the day. Pollsters found young adults had discovered meaningful religious experiences outside the churches. And the mainline bodies could not bring them back. The 1960s had helped to change their values. If they could now no longer be liberationists, they could at least find rewards in expressive ethics. One observer noted, "Many of the faith expressions of nonmembers were more articulate and often more steeped in Christian motifs than comparable statements from church members."[8]

Some spectacular new expressions of being religious showed up in the growing popularity of the "new religions." These focused on exploring the inner life, following one's personal spiritual quest wherever that might lead, in the name of "growth." The best known of these new religious expressions, involving the largest number of seekers, was Transcendental Meditation, to which four percent of the population gave serious attention. Another three percent found in yoga a helpful road to deeper truth. Another two percent professed loyalty to mysticism, and one percent, to Asian faiths.[9]

Added to this was a related movement which started in the 1960s, the "neo-Pentecostal" or "charismatic" renewal among members of mainline Protestant and Roman Catholic churches. Concentrating on utilizing the spiritual gifts of 1 Cor. 12:4-11— especially tongues and their interpretation, healing, and the discernment of spirits—an astonishingly large number of believers flocked to weekly prayer meetings, national renewal conferences, and energetic, small, local groups to share experiences and to probe the meaning of this form of renewal.

The movement clearly reflected the new broadening understanding of being religious. The followers concentrated on intense personal experiences rather than on rational thought and analysis as the principal means of understanding faith. Along with the mystics, they focused on ecstatic experience, on finding larger meanings and new, miraculous energies in their lives through receiving the "second baptism" in which they received one or more of the spiritual gifts. To them, the older understanding of the importance of official doctrine, formal liturgical worship, organized sacramental renewal, and planned parish-education programs were secondary to being religious in their new way. It was new, it was now, and it held the loyalty of millions.

Both the mystics and the charismatics moved away from the activism of the 1960s. Both agreed there would always be wars and rumors of wars. Charismatics agreed with traditionalists that the woman's movement was a direct challenge to the divine order of Ephesians 5, where patriarchal authority was clearly ordained. They also saw the civil rights movement and environmental concerns as diversions from the centrality of discovering and expressing the spiritual gifts. As Joseph H. Fichter explained, the renewed believer "must put everything in the hands of Christ who alone can fashion the good society."[10] He stated that the inner renewal followers "take a miraculous view of social justice, that if all men are brought to Christ social evils will disappear through divine intervention. Thus they concentrate their energies on conversion and evangelism and largely ignore social issues."

Parallel to this new definition was the resurgence of new life among the strongly evangelical and fundamentalist groups. Much of that energy was both a rejection of 1960s activism and expressive ethics, as well as a determined effort to restore "the old-time religion." To them that meant being directly associated with and under the direction of an organized religious authority. From there would come sound doctrinal teachings, absolutist moral norms, and firm direction in social and political controversies.

This resurgence of religious authority was in direct contradiction to what some observers saw as a pervasive trend in American life toward secularity. The conservative resurgence broke out among groups such as Jehovah's Witnesses, Seventh Day Adventists, and the Mormons, evidenced by large membership and financial growth. The stricter a denomination enforced its position, it seemed, the more popular it became for both older and newer members. This was not expected to happen in "post-Christian America."

Such apparent contradictions required careful analysis. This surge was not the result of any large transference of church members from mainline to sectarian bodies. Rather, as Martin E. Marty has suggested, this new traditionalism reflected an antimodernization impulse.[11] The participants were on a nostalgia trip, searching for a more ordered and simpler society. They voiced support for religious pluralism in America, but the bottom line of their quest was national unity under the Christian flag. They used extensive financial and technological know-how to win strong support from single-issue interest groups for their political agenda. All of these forces were energized by their doctrine of the "end times." They believed these were the final days; the rampant amount of sin, evil, vice and satanic activity proved that the devil was ready to bring the world to its knees. Americans no longer enjoyed the luxury of wondering when Armageddon was coming. It was here.

Much of the energy of this new traditionalism was directed into the rough-and-tumble world of American elective politics. In the past these religious conservatives had avoided politics so that they would not have to compromise their vision of absolute truth, or deal with nonbelievers, or take their message into the secular public square. Now they decided that America was so corrupt that it could be saved only by a massive dose of fundamentalist/evangelical righteousness.

Furthermore, career political operatives had detected a rich, untapped reservoir of funds and votes in this conservative camp. During the late 1970s a small but powerful number of fundamentalist leaders in advertising, political lobbying, television, and fund raising decided they must seize the political power of this nation if it were to survive. Skilled spokesmen such as Richard Viguerie, Howard Phillips, and Paul Weyrich built a program to identify the issues, mobilize the masses, and inspire the leadership.[12]

Their case against "godless America" became the agenda for the budding New Christian Right of the next decade. That agenda emerged out of what they detected to be a rampant, if subtle, conspiracy at work destroying America. It was a plot hatched by secular humanists, who were gradually taking control of education, the media, and much of the government. What else could explain the Supreme Court decisions to protect abortions, to ban religious exercises in the public schools, and to show continued opposition to any public support for church-related bodies? What else but an organized conspiracy could explain the continuing demand of women for the Equal Rights Amendment, or explain the antipatriotic thrust of those wanting to appease the communists? What else could explain the galloping rate of increase in drug usage and the greater militancy of homosexuals?

These leaders of the New Christian Right leaders decided the only certain way to reverse all this was to restore America to its rightful Christian origins. That was best done by bringing believers directly into elective politics. The leaders had the funds; they had extensive mailing lists of donors to right-wing, single-issue causes; and they had access to politicians in high places, such as Senators Jesse Helms, Orrin Hatch, and Strom Thurmond, and Governor Ronald Reagan, a candidate for the United States presidency.

Those who wanted to revitalize being religious in America in 1979 created a political action program entitled "The Moral Majority." Its leader was the celebrity television preacher, the Rev. Jerry Falwell of Lynchburg, Virginia, and it concentrated on political education, voter registration, and issues clarification. A similar group in California, named "Christian Voice," added its contribution with "hit lists" of office seekers they wanted to defeat, producing "moral report cards," with carefully chosen issues on which to measure whether the incumbents were for or against morality. The key issues were abortion, the Equal Rights Amendment, religious exercises in public schools, gay rights, and unlimited funding for the Department of Defense. The appeal of the New Christian Right was clear: stand up now and be counted for those leaders who know how to be truly religious, or else forfeit your right to participate in a society which could well collapse.

In the spring and summer of 1980 all of this captured the front-page headlines and the lead news stories of television and radio. This was indeed something new in American political and religious life. Never before had this bloc of citizens entered into the political realm. Never before had their solutions been touted before the general public with such verve and fervor. In November the candidate they endorsed, Ronald Reagan, won the presidency from the incumbent, born-again Jimmy Carter. Several of their targeted incumbent lawmakers on the hit lists were defeated. For the New Christian Right this was proof of divine approval.

What Is at Stake?

In the 35 years of American history since the Second World War, the definition, understanding, and expression of what it means to be religious in America underwent immense change for millions of seekers. What was at stake was the irreconcilable differences among Christians over the extent to which their religious commitments, in contrast to those of their adversaries, were the better informed and biblically sound. Being religious expanded from its church and synagogue-based centers of the 1950s to embrace a huge, often contradictory set of expressions in all areas of religious life. The resulting confusion helped create the increasingly bitter disputes among the many religious "tribes," each bent on preserving its own vision.

Often throughout the course of American history, the rancor and disputation within religious life has swelled and flowed strong, but then receded quickly. That may happen also in our day. But a more likely prospect is that the forces set in motion by the transforming events in America since 1945 will continue to produce conflict. Such conflict should neither be avoided, nor despised. But for it to bear good fruit it should be understood. In the next four chapters, we survey specific ways in which this can occur.

Discussion Questions

1. Recall Naisbett's statement, "The most reliable way to anticipate the future is by understanding the present." Does our understanding of the 1945–1980 era give us a reliable way to anticipate the future? Is the world changing so rapidly as to make our current understanding obsolete?
2. Do you think that the issues of the liberationists— civil rights, women's rights, ecology, and peace— were appropriate issues at that time for the churches to be involved in?
3. Do you find "expressive ethics" consistent with the mission and the teaching of the church?
4. Why did the main direction of American life move away from the liberationist agenda to the more conservative agenda of the 1980s?
5. What was—or is—your attitude toward the New Christian Right?

CHAPTER THREE

Does God Love America Best? Public Faith and Patriotism

During strange and troubled times Americans re-affirm their belief in themselves and their national destiny by celebrating their past. They want to feel good about themselves, and one way to do that is by indulging in old-fashioned, flag-waving patriotism. Nationwide opportunities turned up during the long Bicentennial celebrations of 1976 and the astonishing outpouring of feeling for the return of the hostages from Iran with those yellow ribbons in January 1981.

The best was yet to come. Patriotism burst out everywhere in the summer of 1984; in the traditional Fourth of July celebrations; at the national conventions of Democrats and Republicans; in the growing number of businesses who changed their advertising colors to red, white, and blue; or on the milk cartons of a dairy firm in Washington, D.C., which listed the days we should fly the flag, closing with "any day."

The new national folk hero, Lee Iacocca of Chrysler, seemed the ideal television celebrity to head up the fund-raising drive to pay for fixing up the Statue of Liberty. Rock and roll superstars found enthusiastic encouragement for their pro-American songs and their endorsements of beverages "made the American way." Vietnam veterans, for years ignored or despised, received the classic American endorsement—a ticker-tape blizzard while parading through Manhattan.

Such patriotism needed to connect with the world around it, with the stuff of everyday life. And such stuff was furnished, in star-spangled abundance in the summer of 1984 with the Olympic Games in Los Angeles. President Reagan set the tone when in a national speech he pledged "a future of unlimited promise, an endless horizon lit by the star of freedom guiding America to supremacy."[1]

And what could illuminate that star more than by winning in competitive sports against the world's best, "supremacy" through fair-and-square competition?

A *Time* editor put it this way:

There was a kind of magic about the Games, a brilliance of performance and setting, as if not only the athletes but the place itself and the weather, blue and golden, all rose to the occasion. Sometimes the crowds were gloatingly pro-American as the nation's athletes collected an overachieving 83 gold medals. There was a certain smugly triumphal mood in the stands that replicated the atmosphere of a Reagan campaign rally. At both events, young Americans broke into an overbearing victory chant: "U.S.A.! U.S.A.!" But the

Games also frequently achieved something close to perfection: athletes utterly inhabiting the instant of the act—driving chariots of fire.[2]

As the gold-medal count mounted, the mood helped drive away the United States the fans wanted to forget, that of recession, of Jimmy Carter telling them to lower their expectations, of gas shortages, and hostages crises. Americans were leaving behind those strange and troubled times, moving towards a country where, in the words of their leader, "the future was full of endless possibility." As Lance Morrow put it, "The belief was born that Americans can do—well, *anything.*"[3]

A Covenanted People

But what did this have to do with being religious? What does this resurgence in our day have to do with the deepening crisis over public faith?

Many Americans have believed that, for all its diversity, this nation is truly "a covenanted community, solemnly dedicated to carry out the subordinate to the will of a just God." They believed that such trust would lead the Lord to "favor a community and its prosperity if it remained true to this trust."[4] And the prime responsibility to protect and carry out this mission was given, in the American understanding, to its churches and synagogues.

But, *is that what religious institutions should be all about?* The many angry voices being raised over that issue today help us understand why this adds up to a crisis. The question we consider is as old as humankind, but today it has a special urgency: should governments exist to help make the citizenry better, more religious and moral people? Or, should governments exist to prevent crimes against lives, property, and rights, allowing each citizen the right to pursue his or her own religious commitment?

A Christian Nation?

Perhaps most readers would endorse the latter statement, but as dedicated as we are to pluralism, Americans in the mid-1980s are bitterly divided over whether that freedom depends on ours being a Christian nation. Did we once have a society based on clear, compelling (largely Calvinist) theological absolutes, as the noted spokesman Francis Schaeffer argued? Should our law and public policy be in harmony with the fundamental biblical principles of Judeo-Christian civilization, as Professor Harold O. J. Brown insists?[5]

Or, are the values we cherish more universal, transcending precise definitions? Putting it another way, should our civil law and our Bill of Rights be rooted squarely on Judeo-Christian absolutes? Or should our freedoms rather be considered the result of an age-old struggle between darkness and light? And finally, we must ask: Does that really matter? Does it matter if people such as Schaeffer or Brown, or popular television preachers such as Jerry Falwell, insist that America is, or was, or could be a truly Christian nation?

In this chapter we will insist that it does matter. With the deepening crisis, with Americans locked into battle in the legislatures, courtrooms, and media, we can expect no relief from such struggle unless we understand what is at stake.

Do we want what Grant Wacker has described as a "Christian civilization?"[6] That concept rests on three ideas. First, that certain moral teachings are absolute and that for every moral issue (such as patriotism), there is *always* one final absolute answer. Second, these absolutes must form the visible foundations of our daily laws; that is, those standards we claim for governing our private lives must also regulate our public conduct. Finally, these laws are revealed in nature and in the Bible. Government exists to preserve these absolutes, to make people morally and theologically better.

New Right leaders say there is such a thing as too much freedom—and that is what is wrong with America today. We have too much freedom that allows us to ignore organized religious influences in public life, too much freedom for the media in depicting sex and violence, too much freedom in the public schools to teach antireligious themes such as evolution. For the New Right the antidote is more flag-waving patriotism as a starter, but, more directly, the injection of biblical absolutes directly into public life.

Many Americans, however, refuse to endorse their platform and do so because of their own religious convictions. The battle is over this issue: *Is the Bible a political handbook?* Are there absolute answers there which are so compelling as to leave no room for personal interpretation?

The Bible, the Nation, and Patriotism

The starting point for our search is with the teachings of Jesus towards government. There we have only one direct reference, that of paying tribute to Caesar.[7] Indirectly, Jesus recognized the presence of the state, the authority of its political institutions, and its right to protect order and collect taxes. Jesus accepted civil authority and observed the laws and ordinances. He accepted and obeyed the prescribed Jewish laws. At his trial no evidence was presented to suggest that he was anything less than a model citizen. Pilate wanted to release him.

Jesus used no political power for his mission. Instead, he was in the most profound sense, a "revolutionary," calling for a total transformation of the person and severely condemning the social injustice of the day. That transformation would, of course, help improve the believer's political life, but we have in the four Gospels no blueprint or direct strategy for creating political change.

In the "render to Caesar" statement (Mark 12:17) Jesus taught that the state had claims requiring obedience so long as they did not conflict with the claims made by God. Only God could make claims of eternal worth and demand supreme allegiance. This teaching of Jesus clearly acknowledges the existence of two realms (or kingdoms) and the dual citizenship of the believer to the state and to the kingdom of God. Caesar has his rightful claim, but that does not make him the equal of God. He deserves what is his, but deserves nothing that belongs to God. The state must not be deified; it is never a part of the kingdom.

At his trial Jesus refused to accept the role of political messiah; his loyalties were not with a political nation, but with the kingdom.

The Secular State

Over the centuries political and religious leaders have struggled with the question, How can we be in the world but not conformed to the world? Attempts at creating explicitly Christian nations were made but they were unable over time to hold back the powerful forces of nationalism and secularism. Loyalty to place, to political leaders, to nation proved to be too much for those wanting to have an earthly kingdom which reflected their understanding of God's will. The forces of secularism, through scientific and technological discoveries, and the rise of capitalism served to curb the spread of Christian nations.

Surprisingly, as James E. Wood suggests, "the most effective spokesmen against the notion of the Christian state have come from the churches themselves."[8] Beginning during the 16th-century Reformation, church leaders came to understand that Caesar's realm was that of the secular, while God's realm was that of the sacred. Neither should have governing control over the other; both should remain independent of one another. Most important, a secular state allowed citizens religious liberty to prevent the state from using religious means for the accomplishment of political ends. The secular state would not attempt to promote religion, nor seek to curtail its expression. The presence of the secular state did not mean religion was of secondary importance, only that the best interests of everyone were served when the lines between them were clearly understood and respected.

Wood makes a useful distinction in pointing out that the secular state should not be considered as being hostile to the work of the churches. The secular state is not, or should not be, antagonistic toward religion. It is not the secular state as such that creates the increase in crime, vice, and immorality in a state. At its best the secular state allows each person the opportunity to find his or her own form of religious expression in a state where no official or established church exists. "In matters of religious faith and ultimate belief, the secular state is not committed to atheism, or to secularism, to irreligion or to religion."[9] Wood concludes, "The secular state ought not to be regarded as a barrier but as a benefit to religion."

What does all this mean for the issues of this chapter? By definition *patriotism* is a love for and loyalty to one's country. "For the Christian, patriotism must always be defined in terms of a priority of loyalties. The Christian's first allegiance is to God. Consequently, patriotism can never be defined for the Christian in terms of a supreme allegiance or an ultimate loyalty."[10]

A Lutheran View

That statement is a helpful summation of the issue, as far as it goes. Wood, however, works out of an explicit loyalty to the "free church" tradition. As such, his interpretation is not directly applicable to the full spectrum of the Christian community. Another necessary perspective is added here by looking at the Protestant Reformation tradition, specifically at the doctrine of the two kingdoms or two realms.

Martin Luther saw the mission of the church to be preaching the gospel rather than establishing the kingdom of God on this earth. Through the Word and sacraments, God's presence in this world was made known. Believers lived in this world with its necessary secular authorities alongside its religious leaders. In the medieval setting, those authorities included kings, princes, and emperors, among others. They had the power of the sword, which was clearly distinct from the gospel. They protected life and property and provided justice, and this was by the decree of God.

The kingdom or realm of the sacred was to be kept free from any secular interference. Luther was more willing than the "free church" or Anabaptist tradition to allow for "functional interaction" between church and state, in other words, churches may provide programs and services of broad social benefit, and the government may offer and the churches may accept different forms of assistance to furnish these services. Churches are called on to inform citizens about proposals to advance social justice and human rights. Luther hoped, perhaps unrealistically, that secular authorities would be amenable to the teaching authority of the church. In contrast to the free church tradition, Luther was less optimistic that in any visible sense the kingdom of God could be established in this world. This later led Lutherans to make a rigid separation of the two realms, keeping politics as politics, business as business, while the gospel addressed only spiritual matters. Lutheranism for too long remained silent about secular issues.[11]

Today's renewed discussion over creating a "Christian America" has helped correct that silence. Many citizens speak out against any "Christianization" of society or secularizing of the gospel by replacing it with human programs. The church fulfills its mission when it resists that society which claims to be ultimate, answerable directly and only to God.[12] Both free church representatives and Lutherans have stated the dangers and injustices of uncritical patriotism, of deifying Caesar, and of allowing by default the secular state to use religion for its own purposes. They would perhaps be angry, but not surprised, by the red, white, and blue hoopla, the chants of "U.S.A.," or the easy identification of America's mission in the world with that of the Almighty's. They would remind us that, indeed, the Bible is not a political handbook.

Rituals and Symbols

In the current revival of patriotism is there an overlap (some would say confusion) between nationalist rites and symbols and those of the churches? Is the new patriotism close to becoming a form of idolatry, with the state promising not only to protect the shores from invasion and protect life and property at home, but offering a unifying worldview or set of values that could be called religious?

The reader may well at this point ask a loud, "So what?" Is the singing of the national anthem, or some goosebump feelings at seeing the familiar patriotic symbols, or the invocation of God to bless America really a crisis? Shouldn't the government expect some form of patriotic expression? Once we start neglecting our ceremonies, isn't that the first step toward losing our freedom?

So where's the crisis? The crisis emerges when we expect the government programs, however beneficial, to be a panacea. The crisis also comes when we fail to realize that government leaders, however sincere, can easily use and manipulate religious faith to advance their secular programs. Can we as Americans call on God for direction and inspiration without it serving political ends? Can we show our respect for the liberties and freedoms of this nation without deifying the state that protects them? Where can the two realms, the secular and the sacred, creatively nourish each other?

One such area of common ground is that of our rituals and symbols. From childhood Americans have been involved in expressing our feelings through a variety of solemn, symbol-laden rituals and ceremonies. We learn that specific services, certain physical documents, objects of art, and familiar music all portray our belief in "this nation under God." For some citizens, undoubtedly, these are mere formalities; singing the national anthem before the big game is just one way to rev up. But for many others these observances have a sacred character.

Symbols are substitutes for real and imaginary actions and things, and the relations between them.

They reflect convictions and emotions among humankind about the ultimate problem—the meaning of life. Symbols turn up at the solemn moments of life, such as birth, commencement, rites of passage, marriage, and death. They reassure us that we are keeping faith with our ancestors and our past. We keep them alive for the edification of our children.

A moment's reflection shows us how our religious and patriotic symbols are connected. We are born into the national state, as the believer is born into the church. We are registered as a citizen just as the believer is baptized as a member. We are taught the national "catechism" at school, which upholds the rewards of national loyalty, preparing us for a life of service to the state. Like the Christian church, nationalism has its central physical symbol, the flag. It also is honored with precisely worded rituals of saluting, dipping, and raising. As it passes by, people remove their hats and sing its praises. It receives a daily pledge of allegiance. It has its parades, processions, and pilgrimages, its holy days such as the Fourth of July, Memorial Day, Presidents' Day, and Flag Day. It has temples for its heroes such as the shrines for Washington, Jefferson, and Lincoln. Its heroes are celebrated by being named for national landmarks, parks, or restored homes.

All of these are intended to bring together the American people in a common cause, in a body politic. In the mid-1980s observers noted how the religious and the patriotic were overlapping—in the new fervency in national holiday celebrations, in the political conventions, in the gusto for competing for supremacy, and in support for an unabashedly patriotic president. Beyond that, one expert wrote, there was something close to "the threshold of hysteria. It may not be too extreme to argue that as the organizing symbol of our nation-state and of the Americanism that may be its civil religion, the flag has preempted the place, visually and otherwise, of the crucifix in older Christian lands."[13]

Like the churches, our nationalist rituals have a clearly defined leader. We have agreed that this is the president, the symbolic representative of the whole of the people, all of the states. He leads the rituals and celebrates the virtues of our patriotic faith. We expect him to interpret and legitimize the excruciatingly difficult moral issues facing us. Hence, he has legitimate access to our nationalistic and patriotic symbols, expressed in religious terms.

How wisely and how justly the president uses these powers is a major issue dividing the voters. In the mid-1980s with the new American spirit, President Reagan enthusiastically demonstrated his belief in traditional patriotism as an important expression of faith. This was vividly expressed in the Memorial Day, 1984, services at Arlington National Cemetery, honoring the unknown soldier from the Vietnam war. Some background perspective puts this in focus. An interpreter of the event, W. Lloyd Warner wrote:

> Memorial Day is a cult of the dead which organizes and integrates the various faiths and national and class groups into a sacred unity. It is a cult of the dead organized around the community cemeteries. Its principal themes are those of the sacrifice of the soldier dead for the living and the obligation of the living

to sacrifice their individual purposes for the good of the group, so that they too, can perform their spiritual obligations.[14]

The need for such unity in 1984 was obvious. Vietnam had been America's longest, most controversial war. The symbols and rituals honoring earlier American warriors had been withheld from the survivors of Vietnam. The war itself had become politicized beyond reconciliation.

Into this situation, the president and the appropriate custodians of American religious patriotism brought forward a most remarkable ceremony. The setting at Arlington showed the national television audience its architecture, mirroring that of official Washington. The leaders were the head chaplains of the branches of the Armed Forces: Army, Navy, Air Force, Marine Corps, and Coast Guard. Each offered a prayer or scriptural reading consistent with his particular religious tradition. No denominational symbols were visible. The hymns reflected a careful balance between mainline and evangelical groups: "God of Our Fathers," "Abide with Me," "A Mighty Fortress," "Holy, Holy, Holy," "America the Beautiful," and "Nearer My God to Thee." The Army Chorus sang Psalm 34. The benediction, however, was clearly christological, with references to the risen Christ and the second coming.

Throughout, the president participated as the chief official, concluding the service with the statement about the honored unknown soldier: "He is the heart, the spirit, and the soul of America." The service was a masterful expression of America's blending of patriotism and faith.

What Is at Stake?

The Memorial Day service helped restore a sense of solemnity and finality to the needs we felt about honoring our fallen warriors. It presented a visual outlet for our deepest feeling, revealing how such ceremonies could remind us of the transcendent meaning of life. Yet these moments of unity are precious few. Most of our daily lives are inevitably filled with more mundane activities.

So we ask, first, how can we infuse the best of our religious convictions with the best of our responsibilities as citizens? How can we be patriotic without being idolatrous? Might such a situation develop if, as the Rev. Jerry Falwell exhorted, "It is time for Americans to come back to the faith of our fathers, and to the biblical principles that our fathers used as a premise for this nation's establishment"? Would we be the better off if we followed the advice of Moral Majority vice-president Tim LaHaye to elect "promoral leaders who will return our country to the biblical base upon which it was founded"? What would most likely be the result if we wrote into law the political planks of the Moral Majority? Such groups have every right to exist and contend earnestly, which they do. Such groups, however, like every other lobby, need to stand under constant scrutiny when they claim theirs is the only true way to the kingdom.

Second, it is well to remember that the idea of a "Christian nation" is essentially a contradiction in terms. Since the time of Christ, we have not had any nation chosen by God. Furthermore, the rather rationalistic faith of many of the founding fathers raises serious questions about how "Christian" (as we understand the term today) they wanted the ideology and institutions of government to be.[15]

Third, what can be wrong for believers to "return to the Bible"? The answer is, of course, that we should return to the Bible every day. But we live in a society that is religiously pluralistic; we have our civic as well as our churchly citizenship. That should lead us to conclude that when acting in our civic, secular capacities, we should not appeal exclusively to religious authority. We do not do so in, say, criminal law cases. George Marsden reminds us, "In a murder trial one cannot appeal to a special revelation to provide an exonerating circumstance. In the court, as in much of civic activity, we can leave our Bibles closed and yet find means of expressing biblically informed truths according to rules on which persons of various religions can agree."[16]

Fourth, might it not be helpful to remember as Paul Simmons reminds us that "America is not a Christian country, but a country in which many Christians happen to live"?[17] Christians must not claim special privilege or power because of their faith, but faith surely calls us to a sense of special responsibility. Might the fervent expressions of patriotism suggest that we know God is on our side, and since God cannot be divided, he is not on the side of those with whom we are contesting? To do so would be to substitute our nationalistic pride for Christian teaching.

Fifth, we return at the end to where we started: what is patriotism? Two versions give us direction. One is by Professor Larry Rasmussen, a student of the life and thought of Dietrich Bonhoeffer. He wrote,

"Whatever else true Christian patriotism is, it is a profound acceptance—not in the sense of uncritical affirmation, with or without the bravado of 'supremacy.' But acceptance in its genuine sense, 'to take on,' 'to receive willingly'. . . . What is taken on, as one's own, is both the culture's gifts, to cherish, to pass on, and responsibility for its cries and victims, to atone for, to deter, to prevent. Community, solidarity, and sacrifice—these are the values of Christian patriotism."[18]

And with a direct American motif, we receive direction from the words of Richard Evans, speaking in Salt Lake City on July 4, 1971:

How Much Is All This Worth?

We the People. Perhaps we the people should ask ourselves, as Daniel Webster once did: "How much is all this worth?" How much is it worth to live where one wishes? How much is it worth to have the right to live with loved ones? to listen to the laughter of children? to walk home and find loved faces unafraid? How much is it worth to own personal property? to have personal privacy? to preserve human dignity? How much is it worth to have an education offered everyone? How much is it worth freely to express an opinion, freely to move from place to place, with an openness of life, with peace of mind and quiet conviction and enjoyment of the great and good earth that God has given? Despite some encroachments on freedom, and the unwise relinquishment of some rights, still blessed beyond belief, still precious beyond price, is the freedom our forebears paid for—the freedom which is God-given, but which yet has to be earned, over and over again. *How much is all this worth?* It must be worth the willingness to work, to serve, to live with loyalty and allegiance, with respect for self, for others, for life, for law, for loved ones, with cleanliness and honorable conduct. Thank God for liberty and for the Constitution of our Country. No nation ever had its equal in making possible the full, free living of life. And we who are living on the short side of life are earnestly anxious that you who have longer yet to live may know, as Andrew Jackson said it, that "No free government can stand without virtue in the people, and a lofty sense of patriotism." Oh, let us turn our thoughts to the character of our country, so that we the people and *our* children and *their* children may thankfully say, "Thank God my life has been spent in a land of liberty."[19]

Discussion Questions

1. Are you inspired when participating in traditional forms of patriotic expression? Does it seem religious?
2. What are your memories of the 1984 Olympic games?
3. "America is a Christian nation." Do you agree or disagree?
4. If the Bible is *not* a political handbook, can it help us in trying to be better citizens?
5. Which of America's problems would be relieved if we became a Christian nation?
6. What is a Christian patriot?

CHAPTER FOUR

Pluralism:
Finding the Boundaries
for Religious Freedom

In a nation that justly prides itself on protecting an immense variety of religious expressions, few events could match that of the trial of the Rev. Sun Myung Moon and his Unification Church in the early 1980s. Consider these facts:

1. Moon came from an uneducated peasant family in Korea.

2. The sacred book of the church he founded, titled *Divine Principle,* is, two experts say, "a bizarre mixture of pseudo-science, numerology, Korean shamanism, and evangelical Christianity."[1]

3. The book teaches that a second messiah, the Lord of the Second Advent, will come from Korea to complete the unfinished ministry of Jesus Christ. Moon's followers believe he is that figure.

4. His church, deeply entrenched in Korea and Japan, gives to its leaders between 70 and 100 million dollars a year for its ministry.[2]

57

5. The best estimate of the total number of full-time disciples of Rev. Moon in the United States is between 5000 and 7000.

6. He first attracted national publicity in the early 1970s for claiming Richard Nixon was God's gift to save the world from communism.[3]

7. He has been repeatedly charged and taken to court for allegedly turning earnest young adult converts into mindless, zealous zombies.

8. He has been charged by the federal government and convicted of income tax evasion.

9. As the implications of his trial became known nationally, he received support through several *amicus curiae* (friends of the court) briefs to help persuade the appeals courts to acquit Rev. Moon. These included Roman Catholic bishops, the National Council of Churches, Moral Majority, Christian Voice, the National Association of Evangelicals, the African Methodist Episcopal Church, the Southern Christian Leadership Conference, the American Civil Liberties Union, the National Bar Association, the Church of Jesus Christ of Latter-Day Saints, the American Association of Christian Schools, the National Conference of Black Mayors, The Presbyterian Church, U.S.A., The American Baptist Churches in the U.S., the Christian Legal Society, and other similar organizations.[4]

Putting these items together may well lead us to conclude it could happen "only in America." That familiar phrase may well help us understand how so controversial a group of religious seekers could win such heartfelt support from the leaders of organized religion in this country. And this trial, occurring "only in America," leads us to raise some questions over the deepening crisis that the new religions and extreme religious pluralism raise for us today.

The Question We Consider

1. If it is true that a nation has no more religious freedom than the degree to which it allows its most deviant believers to flourish, then how far are we willing to go to protect that freedom? Do we want to redefine the boundaries?

2. How can the rewards of active participation in mainline religious life be made more compelling to the largest absentee group from those churches—the young adults?

3. What are, or should be, the limits on the extent to which seekers can claim freedom of expression of religion when their actions violate the law?

Affirmations

Perhaps the most helpful way to go about exploring these questions would be for me to make some personal affirmations.

1. Religious freedom, the celebration of this vast diversity of religious life we heard praised in Chapter 1, flourishes because the United States is a secular state, not an established religious state. As founding father James Madison envisioned it, the state is independent of the church or ecclesiastical control, and the churches are independent of state or political control.

2. The religious pluralism that such freedom creates is not the same thing as secularism. In a secular

state we do not reject faith. Many people today cannot understand that. They would tolerate dissenter groups, but would also insist that ours is a nation based on specific religious absolutes—the ones from their own particular religious tradition.

3. Americans reject the new religions, such as the Unification Church, not so much for their theology, but because those bodies are so communal and collectivist. Most Americans prefer a more individualistic and privatized faith. For example, Unificationists met hostility because outsiders thought they were attempting to undermine both American youth and, eventually, American freedom. Unification doctrine was not at stake.[5]

4. Mainline churches often fail to attract or hold adults because these churches do not teach that the joys and rewards of religious life require dedication and sacrifice—which many adults are willing to make.

The Coming of the New Religions

What, then, is the deepening crisis in pluralism? How did we get into such a situation?

We start by defining some terms. The first is *cults*. Are cults groups such as Jim Jones and Peoples' Temple? Or are cults smooth-talking radio preachers foretelling the end of the world but in the meantime asking you to please send in your monthly pledge? Or are cults composed of worshipful converts devoted to a charismatic leader who claims new religious insights and powers and full control over their lives?

Specialists differ widely over precise definitions, because each of them sees a different part of the whole. Some use the term *cult* in a critical manner; any cult is *ipso facto* dangerous, or at least wrong. Others see these bodies as the beginning of an entirely new direction in world religion. The participants are willing to make a radical break with existing religious communities in favor of something totally new. Other observers suggest that cults are simply new church bodies being formed, which is in harmony with the great tradition of American religious innovation.

What I say is this: For all their differences, the cults that appeared in the last two decades—the Unification Church, Scientology, the Children of God, The Way International, Hare Krishna, and Divine Light Mission—do have several features in common. Ronald Enroth summarizes:

> Most such groups respect their leaders highly. The Moonies border on deification. They depart from revealed truth, false teaching. As a sociologist, I see an adversarial stance *vis a vis* the social institutions of our society. There is also a degree of control at work, not only in the Eastern religions or more exotic cult groups, but also in some groups that claim to be evangelical. Most such groups believe, too, that they are in some way exclusively correct and superior to all other faiths.[6]

These groups offer their followers an all-encompassing way of living which becomes strongly critical of mainline values. Made up largely of younger adults, the new religions create new family structures and loyalties within their own ranks, often at the expense of ties to their families of origin. The new religious seekers participate in extended communal relationships, including shared earnings and property. They devote intensive energies and much time recruiting new members and raising funds. They have created new symbol systems and liturgies for their worship, emphasizing group and ecstatic forms of expression.

All of these qualities elicit the hostility and criticisms of the larger society. One observer chastises "their frequent messianic intolerance and their lack of community and grass-roots support."[7] They have chosen to repudiate those religious and social values most Americans cherish, such as the nuclear family, private property, and the traditional church. Thus they become religious in ways that are not traditionally middle-class American.

Their presence creates a problem, bordering on a crisis, because they are not simply some oddball, misfit unstable "weirdos" waiting for the next fad to join. Instead, the recruits are largely young, stable adults of the educated, professional, white middle class in all sections of the country.

Those who study the new religions disagree, however, over the extent to which the recruits understand the traditional religions they are rejecting. Enroth and Melton write that "some 80–85% of the people who join cults come from non-religious or nominally religious homes."[8] But another watcher, Walter Martin, states that "seventy-eight percent of people who are today in cults came out of professing Christian churches."[9]

Altogether, some 5000 new religions—ranging from a handful of seekers to groups with several thousand members—flourish in the United States. They have the funds, the energy, and the vision to continue their programs for the foreseeable future. As such, they stand in judgment of the major denominations, a judgment intensified not only by their considerable resources but by their apparently strange, often nonconformist expressions of faith. Such behavior provokes resistance.

Perhaps the greatest lure they possess is their ability to offer emotional rewards and the fulfillment of personal needs, qualities which the mainline denominations often fail to provide. Younger seekers criticize the existing churches for not really practicing what they preach. They also claim that the mainline churches are too shallow. Their indictment reads something like this: The mainliners lack an outreach to the oppressed and ignored; their spirituallity seems superficial; they fail to create a sense of warmth and acceptance.[10]

The new religions offer programs that apparently meet the personal needs of these seekers. The leader serves as a father figure, the group becomes a surrogate family, and the daily routine becomes a welcome ordering of life. Enroth reports that new members state "they valued being a part of a group that was doing something important. Moonies have told me they couldn't care less about Rev. Moon's doctrines and that they would probably have left if they hadn't made such good friends."[11] Surely, then, the changing definition of religion and this form of expressive ethics have brought on the crisis we are exploring here.

Unificationism

Some observors of the new religions disagree with my contention we have a crisis here. They point out that the number of participants is extremely small, that the Unification Church has no more than 7000 members, and similar groups acknowledge a high turnover rate.[12] Furthermore, these observers state, the "cult phenomenon" is really a media event created by television and exposé journalists for its human interest and visual appeal.

Another argument is also raised. Don't such groups serve as a safety valve, attracting those people who wouldn't do well anyway in the competitive, young, upwardly mobile world of today's America? Where's the harm? If those 2000 folks in rural Oregon who like to wear orange pajamas and worship a nonverbal guru who likes to ride around in a Rolls Royce, and they all stick to their own turf, why not? The statistics show that over 90% of those who join a new religion return home within two years.[13] So why all the fuss? Those who did remain found themselves the dupes of an imposter who was finally forced to leave Oregon and the United States by state and federal officials.

To answer these criticisms and to address the questions raised at the start of this chapter, we will look more closely at the Unification Church. In the last 15 years it has been the most controversial of all new bodies, and to this day its programs raise important questions for us. Furthermore, the Unificationists or "Moonies" stand out because they seek to influence national public policy and because they have substantial financial resources.[14]

Why all of this occurred is not easily summarized. In my estimation, Rev. Moon attracted very strong support at the beginning in the United States because of his appealing vision of the one Unificationist world family. He took that vision directly into the American political world during the early 1970s, calling on America to be the unrelenting leader in a spiritual and militaristic sense to stop atheistic communism. The Unification Church openly (and legally) spent huge sums to persuade the public to support the anticommunist foreign policy of President Nixon. But to many Americans that seemed an unwarranted intrusion by a foreigner into domestic politics.

The Unificationists also received sharp criticism for their theology. After a careful study by a research team, the National Council of Churches of Christ concluded that such teachings were not Christian. Similar conclusions were reached by Japan's Catholic Bishops and the French Episcopal Conference.[15] Coupled with that were the stories from ex-Moonies, the dropouts from recruitment programs. They told the media of Unificationist demands for submission to the leaders, of coercive spiritual and physical discipline and routine, of intense fasting and prayer, of being required to sell flowers in public centers for very long periods, of being forced to ignore their families and former friends. Most Americans looked critically at the mass marriages, prepared in the traditional Korean manner by the Rev. Moon himself.[16] All in all, this new religion seemed no way for Americans to express their faith.

By way of reply, the Unificationists started to spend very large amounts of money to build respectability among professional groups. They sponsored conferences among scientists, college teachers, and ministers to explain their cause and to win good will. These were held at posh hotels, with all the participants receiving full funding for transportation, room, and board. No other new religious body had such resources. Critics argued this was no way to win respectability. And the money, coming largely from the gifts of members of Asian churches, gave the Unification Church, some said, an unfair advantage over the voluntaristic activities of the North American churches.

Despite strong criticism, the Unificationists continue to pursue their stated objectives. They have moved directly into mainstream American political life with the purchase and management of the *Washington Times,* a daily newspaper. From the outset, the editors made it clear they sought to influence American policy making, especially to make it more actively resistant to any form of what they perceived as communist expansion overseas or at home. The *Times* also directed programs to raise funds for clothing, food, and medicine for the *contra* army in Nicaragua in the mid-1980s. Another Unificationist program in the political arena gave some $500,000 to fund a political-religious action program, the Coalition for Religious Freedom, which focused on supporting political office seekers who support Unificationist positions on church/state issues. Part of that fund was sent to another political lobby, created during the 1984 presidential campaign, the Americans Concerned for Traditional Values (see p. 87).[17] Other Unificationist money, some $3,500,000 was spent to send books, cassettes, tapes, and other printed information to a variety of organized religious bodies, especially to ministers.

All of this proves to be very controversial for many Americans. Yet, paradoxically, while this was occurring many religious leaders from every cluster of doctrinal, ethnic, and regional loyalties supported the right of Rev. Moon to pursue his programs. For all his upsetting qualities, Rev. Moon was seen by these leaders as less a threat to religious pluralism than was the ongoing harassment and intimidation they felt was being directed at him by the Internal Revenue Service (IRS). This harassment, however well-intentioned, could destroy religious freedom in this country, they believed.

The issue even today is extremely complicated and volatile. After several years of deliberations over the finances of the Unification Church, the IRS brought the church to trial, claiming Rev. Moon had failed to pay taxes on $162,000 in income from stocks and a bank account. Moon replied that he was not liable for taxes, because the assets belonged not to him personally, but were held in trust for the church. His attorney, Lawrence Tribe, failed to convince the first trial jury. Eventually the case worked its way up through appeals courts, but was denied a hearing by the Supreme Court. At stake was the money deposited in a New York bank allied with an import firm called Tong II Enterprises. The Unification Church argued this was under the direction of the church, and no personal profits were involved.

By the time the highest court refused to take it on appeal, the case had turned into a celebrated cause. Rev. Moon received support from the leaders and groups listed above. In general the following points were made. Rev. Moon had requested a bench trial (a trial before a judge) rather than a jury trial, but was refused. Second, a government agency (here, the IRS) should not be permitted to dictate the manner in which churches take care of their internal funding and use their own funds. The way such funds were spent was based on the specific content of the doctrines of the church. Thus, since every church enjoyed the freedom to pursue its own doctrine, it should have the attendant right to spend its funds as it sees fit. Third, many churches deposit church funds (obviously these are tax exempt) in the name of the local minister. Fourth, in the Roman Catholic church the property is often held in the name of the local bishop; the Unificationists were asking for the same right. Finally, as Tribe argued, the guaranteed constitutional right to the free exercise of religion was being threatened. By that he meant that when the courts are allowed to define the content of the doctrine, by dictating the manner in which funds are spent, they are assuming powers which are unconstitutional. Only the members of a church when acting in good faith should be allowed to define what they believe, and the courts must recognize that as a valid form of organized religion. Tribe summarized the matter; if church leaders who follow the advice of their people and for such are sent to jail, "they will indeed be the first religious leaders since the ratification of the Constitution to be imprisoned because of the way they and their followers chose to organize their church's internal affairs."[18]

The federal government's case was less complicated, declaring that "to look at the quality of a taxpayer's proof hardly violates the First Amendment." While "a church is free to organize itself as it sees fit, religious leaders, no less than the average taxpayer, must assume the risk when they engage in undocumented transactions that the jury may not believe their account of the events."[19] In the eyes of the prosecution, religious bodies should not enjoy special protections not granted to other citizens engaged in business activities. The IRS is suspicious of those leaders who claim they have no personal interest at stake. American religious history has been replete with examples of ministers who used their flock's funds for their personal benefit. The courts here accepted the government's contention that a significant difference existed between "the religious" on the one hand and "the economic" on the other.

That was, in essence, at the heart of the case: What did it mean to be religious? The government, the IRS, and the courts held for the separation of the religious from the economic sphere. A very large portion of the organized religious and legal communities held to another set of convictions. That is close to being a crisis.

What Is at Stake?

How far are we willing to go to protect religious pluralism? How do we respond to the full extent of that diversity? Do we support the rights of everything and everyone from *A*rica Mind Control to *Z*en Buddhism? Do we celebrate being *A*mish, *B*aptist, *C*ongregational, *D*isciples, and down to *Z*oroastians? Do we consider this diversity a sign of God's providence? Or would we feel better if they were members of our churches? Do we believe our hymns are better, our teachings more sound, our social outreach better balanced with our spirituality? In short, where do our judgments begin and end? On what basis do we justify criticizing others?

Are these new religions trends or fads? They do reflect clearly some of the new momentum for religious living which came out of the 1960s. They are a form of "religious populism," a movement characterized by an emphasis on the promotion of faith for mass audiences. The new religions fit into that movement with their diversity and fluidity, holding high the needs of the individual seeker and ignoring the programs of the mainline bodies.[20]

Their presence also suggests how shortsighted those critics were who had predicted that our society was moving steadily towards total secularization. We were told that religious faith was soon to be replaced by more intelligence and mature morality. We were to celebrate "secular man" and the "secular city." Today the new religions help remind us of the innate religious dimension of our human spirits.

Commendable as those qualities are, we must look more concretely at the *kind* of religion the new groups promote. Three features stand out: (*a*) using their highly privatized authority leader, they emphasize more of a mystical union than a rational involvement in our society; (b) they concentrate on involvement with their immediate peer group rather than reaching boldly to meet the needs of victims of injustice and oppression; (c) they accept the reward system of individualistic capitalism; that is, their members live communally, while their money comes from the wealth amassed by a few persons.

To be concrete, is Lowell D. Streiker, a student of new religions, on the right track when he points to the Unificationists as an organization being in disarray, pouring "millions of dollars down the drain" and unable to hold on to recruits? Even though good public relations is as American as our favorite pie, isn't so much emphasis on public relations an unwise use of resources?

We are reluctant, however, to allow any person outside of a religious group to decide how it should spend its money. Dean M. Kelley answers: "How a religious body raises, invests and expands its funds cannot be divorced from its religious purposes, ministry and mission, and Government cannot intervene in the one without affecting the other."[21] That is a part of what is at stake.

What about the charges of deprogramming and brainwashing? What of the parents who tell of their children being lost to groups who use systematic forms of mind manipulation? At the same time, what of those seekers who tell the public they have been kidnapped by professional anticult ideologues, treated to round-the-clock deprogramming, and forced to return to a society they had chosen to leave?

For several reasons, this controversy today lacks the intensity it generated a decade ago. First, the courts generally have ruled in favor of young adults, of legal age, who join and participate in the religious groups of their choices. Legislatures, by and large, have struck down pro-deprogramming proposals which would give preemptive rights to parents over their recalcitrant children. Second, at least the best-known new religions have softened or modified some of the earlier, more aggressive and objectionable re-cruiting and indoctrination practices. The Unifica-tionists, for example, admit that their house in Oak-land, California, was carrying on some practices of mind-bending as charged by dropouts and parents; corrective practices were taken. At the mass wedding of over 2000 Unificationist couples in 1982 in Mad-ison Square Garden, the officials made sure the par-ents of the newlyweds were in attendance and com-municating with their children. Finally, several civil libertarian groups and individual attorneys have made available their services to those who find they need legal counsel after they decide to leave a specific new religion.

What Can We Do?

What can those of us in the pews do? It isn't enough to study about the new religions, or send letters to our lawmakers about appropriate legislation.

We can, first of all, do something often overlooked. We can witness for our faith to those among the new religions and to our friends. There are those who avoid such witnessing because of what Walter Martin has called the "disease of non rock-a-boatus ecclesiasticus—which disdains controversy."[22] Instead of promoting ease and nicety, churches would minister better by encouraging full discussion in major matters of faith.

Second, we can ask our public school officials to start or to improve the many curricular programs in world religions and religious literature. Very often, misunderstanding about the new religions comes from a lack of information. Schools can teach religious studies without these courses being turned into indoctrination.

Third, in both our schools and in congregational study programs, more attention can be given to exploring how related fields of learning can help us understand what it means to be religious. Cultural anthropology, sociology, and psychology offer rich insights into the issues we are exploring in this book.

Fourth, we can encourage our seminary leaders to keep the curriculums of their respective schools in harmony with parishioners' needs and interests. Knowing that the role of the parish minister is becoming increasingly fragmented and complex, we want to send a message to religious educators for the need to maintain a balance between studying the foundations of the faith and the many ways in which our society uses that faith.

Fifth, as suggested by new religions specialists J. Gordon Melton and Robert L. Moore, congregations need to periodically assess their ministries to teens and young adults. Very often, it seems, churches accept as unchangeable the demographic evidence that people within those age groups will stay away from church. The popularity of the new religions proves that to be wrong. Might there be an extensive broadening of social outreach programs such as Lutheran Volunteers or the Mennonite volunteer program for young adults, which gives special attention to spiritual nurture and social activism?[23] Such programs exist, but are reaching only a few. Melton and Moore have stated, "If we in mainline Protestant churches do not help our young people by modeling a serious commitment to a life-affirming religion vision and praxis, then we should not be surprised that others step into the vacuum we in our smugness have created."[24] Not all young adults want to become Yuppies; some are ready for entering the world of sacrificial service. We need to find them

Sixth, churches and families can concentrate more on helping older teens prepare themselves for the time they will leave the immediate family. That preparation will require more research and creative program-building than we have now to smooth the transition. The possibilities for planners here and in all the programs listed in this chapter are limited only by the imagination of the planners.

Seventh, we can face more fully the question: Can there be too much religious freedom? The courts have already established some clear boundary lines. Those who attempt in the name of faith to deny blood transfusions to their children have been overruled by the courts upholding the primary right of the state to protect life. Parents cannot let their young sons or daughters stand at dangerous street corners at night to distribute religious literature. The handing round of poisonous snakes in the name of proving God's protection is illegal. So too is polygamy and the use of hallucinogens in organized religious worship. These are some examples of government regulation of religion.

The government has stepped in to protect citizens against fraud, embezzlement, kidnapping, and other such felonies whose perpetrators have claimed religious freedom as their defense. But, acknowledging that, what would we say to a young adult who is considering joining the Salvation Army or a Trappist monastery? Professor William J. Whalen has posed a compelling problem: What of the young man "who forsakes his family and friends to affiliate with a religious movement, sleeps five or six hours a day, denies himself sexual activity, lives on a diet largely bereft of meat or fish and turns over any income he receives to the head of his group?"[25] Is that any different from what today's new religions require?

Understanding the new pluralism can help us see what is involved when someone close to us looks favorably on a new religion. This religious exploration is filled with risk, some danger, and inevitable tension. Controversy and disappointment are bound to occur. By no means can the strains and stresses of this deepening crisis be eliminated or even sharply reduced. But when we see this exploration for what it is, we can view it as part of God's providential care.

Discussion Questions

1. What limits would you place on religious pluralism in the United States? What should *not* be allowed?

2. Should church revenue be exempt from scrutiny by the Internal Revenue Service?
3. What would you do if your daughter or son started attending a program of one of the new religions?
4. Is being a Unificationist any different from being a Trappist monk or joining the Salvation Army?
5. Do you agree that the church lacks appeal for the highly idealistic young adult?
6. Should it change its programs to attract this group? How might it do that?

CHAPTER FIVE

Public Policy Making and the Churches: A New Agenda?

When we choose to express our faith in public, we are choosing to become political. We are choosing to get involved in the lives and destinies of other people. That means we must make choices about how we want to live our lives together. To do that we need leaders, we need agreed-on ways of solving our common problems, and we need ways to decide how we like the policies we have chosen. That is what I mean by being political.

In recent years that is becoming increasingly complicated to do. We have, everyone agrees, some kind of a crisis on our hands. This is intensified because of our growing tendency to do battle for what we want in public policy on the basis of our own tribal needs—our economic, regional, gender, or age-related loyalties. Yet while we do that, we acknowledge that our religious faith compels us to uphold that which

77

is beyond tribalism, that which is absolute and eternal. This is one way of defining our crisis.

Do We See What We Want to See?

Once we decide our faith is public, we run into controversy. We encounter disagreement, not only from those who do not share our faith but often from close friends. In other words, our efforts to be religious do not necessarily unite us; indeed, those efforts are often the source of our divisions.

To illustrate this dilemma we will look at a specific situation, of specific people, all of whom were acting religiously but who ran into conflict. In November 1984, 12 Lutheran women participated in a 14-day seminar conducted in Mexico, El Salvador, and Nicaragua sponsored jointly by the American Lutheran Church and the Center for Global Service and Education of Augsburg College. Several such seminars had already been carried out by these institutions. The program brochure stated that the seminar would "introduce participants to the reality of poverty and injustice in Latin America," "examine the root causes of these problems," and "reflect on our responsibilities as Christian women in alleviating hunger while working for social and political change."[1] It was a superb example of the blending of religion and politics.

The women spent five days in Cuernavaca, three in El Salvador, and six in and around Managua, Nicaragua. They met with a wide variety of people: farmers, government officials, factory workers, teachers, church workers, and others. On their return home four of the 12, in pairs, submitted their reactions to the ALC periodical, *The Lutheran Standard*. One pair found the gospel of Jesus Christ at the center of the programs working for social and economic reform. These two participants looked at "the reality of poverty through the eyes of the poor as a faithful response to Christ's call to seek truth, justice and peace."[2] They felt their church should continue to support the kind of grass-roots involvement they found there to help relieve the poverty and seek justice as a faithful response to God's commands.

The other pair of women found both the program and most of the leaders they met "calculated to convince participants that the cause of Nicaragua's Marxist Sandinistas and El Salvador's guerillas is just and morally pure, while U.S. policy is oppressive and the single cause of the region's problems." They concluded, "as good Christians, we were encouraged to return home and organize opposition to U.S. policy."[3] To them the combined religion-and-politics program increased class hatred and limited God's love to only one part of that society. The total impact, in their estimate, was an attempt by the ALC and the Augsburg Center "to politicize the altruistic sentiments of sincere but gullible Americans, not so much to help the suffering as to support an alien political doctrine that is anything but altruistic."

In the first team one woman stated she had in the late 1960s become politically active in the civil rights and antiwar movements. One woman in the second team wrote that she had been for a time actively involved in the John Birch Society, "an organization that sees pervasive communist influence in our society."[4]

Does that lead us to conclude that people see what they want to see? that they bring their long-standing tribal loyalties to new interactions of religion and politics? that we cannot really overcome such deep-rooted commitments? Those are the kinds of questions we confront when we try to see how our faith speaks to us in the realm of political involvement.

The temptation here is to conclude that we really do see just what we want to see, that our faithful response to God's commands depends on our own interests. But does that have to be the case? Are we so locked into our own worlds that we lose sight of just how transforming and demanding our faith can be? Have we overlooked the possibility that our organized communities of faith, our churches, can lead us beyond our tribal loyalties?

The Role of the Churches

The response of these women raises for us a question: *Is there any good reason to believe the churches can make a significant difference in our public and political lives?* The information we have to answer that question is not especially encouraging. For example, the Gallup Poll study of *Religion in America, 1984,* raised serious questions for the churches.[5] It concluded that while "religion is growing in importance among Americans ... morality is losing ground." Much the same conclusion was reached by the Roper Poll and *U.S. News & World Report* study in late 1985. The most serious signs of growing immorality were found in increasing organized crime, drug and alcohol abuse, corporate and labor union dishonesty, cheating on income taxes, and child abuse.

Yet, at the same time, interest in religion seemed to be on the increase. Church attendance slowly moved up. Americans expressed more confidence in the church as a reliable social institution than in the government, the courts, or big business. Those polled stated that the churches were the places where they encountered God directly, studied the Bible, and interacted with other believers. Gallup concluded: "We are in a period of enormous opportunity for the churches of this nation and the challenge immediately ahead is clearly that of recognizing and understanding this interest, tapping this interest, and forming it into solid religious commitment. There is a certain urgency about this."[6] In other words, we are in a deepening crisis.

But what kind of crisis? Why should we believe this is any different from the dilemmas of earlier times? Can't we just accept the fact that people, like the four travelers to Central America, will see what they want to see, that the churches will always be in the dilemmas Gallup describes, and that we should continue to go about our own ways of life?

To answer those questions we need to remember, first, that both as citizens and as church members we are free at any time to abstain from direct political involvement. Our participation is always voluntary. So, too, with our religious organizations. Their spokespersons are free to choose whether to extend their ministries into the shaping and enforcement of public policy. We remember also that throughout American history some churches have been highly political, seeking to bring the kingdom to this earth largely through political means. On the other hand, some churches have concentrated exclusively on renewing the inner life of the believer. The choice is ours.

We need, secondly, to remember that in our nation's past the record of political involvement by churches in shaping public policy has been, by and large, a failure to achieve their stated goals. In pre-Civil War America, for example, devout church people on both sides of the Mason-Dixon line prayed to the same God, read the same Bible, and involved themselves as believers in the issue over the abolition of slavery. The political means for that abolition, endorsed by the churches, failed. Slavery finally disappeared only after military intervention. Years later, many devout church people attempted to outlaw the production, sale, and consumption of alcoholic beverages; and many equally devout believers opposed the Prohibition movement. And, of course, Prohibition failed.

Private or Social?

Both failures reflect the heart of the problem over why and how the churches should involve themselves in public life. The problem can be stated this way: If, as some observers insist, our moral lives as well as our religion are private, a matter of personal preference, then the churches have no authority or even any need to help instruct or lead their people in public issues. But if our morality and religion are public, if the churches have "good reasons, coherent ideals, and true examples, then the churches have the authority and need to carry out such leadership. The churches can help us understand what the great public issues mean in light of the Scriptures, in the life of Jesus, in the laws of nature, and the kingdom of God. That is what religious institutions should be helping us to learn."[7]

But doesn't that in some way violate what Americans believe is the "separation of church and state"? Aren't the two realms to be kept separate? The answer to that is not a simple yes or no. Nowhere in our history or our Constitution is a total isolation of church and state from each other required. The record shows that the churches have been and are now a highly important part of public policy making in the United States.

Why is that important? The gospel is located in God's power made manifest in history and available to us. Christians are to use that power in this world, "as instruments of God's divine purpose for his creation."[8] The gospel is "power," the expression of that gospel. That power is to be "light" or "salt" or "leaven," giving the church its mission to the world. Unless the gospel is that power, it is not true to its source.

By taking its mission seriously, James Wood has asserted, the church should "take seriously the evil in the world, in both people and institutions and it must always seek to advance God's kingdom of justice and righteousness."[9] The church should preach justice and be a force for justice in the world. It must avoid allying itself with any institution, such as the government, that would mute its prophetic voice. But it should be ready to apply the gospel as its mission to the world. Unless the church does this, it faces its "greatest danger today, the widespread tendency of the church to support the status quo, militant nationalism, and power structures identified with injustice and oppression."[10]

"Black theologians have rightly reminded us in recent years, 'If God is not the God of the oppressed he is not the God of the New Testament.' "[11] Walter Rauschenbusch wrote that "Ascetic Christianity called the world evil and left it. Humanity is waiting for a revolutionary Christianity which will call the world evil and change it."[12]

But, on the other hand, isn't it possible that the churches will get too deeply involved in the matters of this world? How can we protect against that? How can we find some balance? The answer to that is not so evident that everyone will agree on it. First of all, just as God created the church as an instrument of his will on earth, so God created human institutions such as the government (and families, schools) for the ordering of our lives. God is working in all those organizations that sustain our everyday lives, and that includes our public and political lives. In other words, in our worry over getting too involved in this world, we should remember God's purposes are often carried out *in* this world, *by* this world's institutions.

Second, God's purposes are carried out when government rewards good behavior and punishes wrongdoing. When our political leaders do that, and when we obey them, we are helping in bringing God's power to earth.

Third, this means that all of us, in our roles as citizens, should be watchful that our governments do not do wrong. By criticizing our public policy leaders we are helping them and our society keep good order.[13] When we decide to do that, we decide to follow what we think is best. And that is where we sometimes find our fellow Americans disagreeing with us.

The Issues Today

Why now, in the mid-1980s, is all this so pressing an issue? It becomes important because we have seen a major public controversy erupt over the issue of "religion and politics." Generally, this is attributed to two causes: the appearance of the so-called "New Christian Right" and the endorsement by President Ronald Reagan of an explicitly polemical outlook on the issue. Further, both causes have roots and find support in the new patriotism we considered in Chapter 3.

This has become controversial because the New Christian Right is often polemical, argumentative, and judgmental toward those who see the relation between religion and politics in a light different from theirs. It is also controversial because President Reagan changed the traditionally nonsectarian approach of American presidents regarding theological judgments about American public life. Until Reagan's administration, presidents had made very generally worded, broadly nonsectarian policy statements on the need for high moral standards and devotion to the ideals of the Judeo-Christian tradition. Presidents issued rather blandly worded proclamations for Thanksgiving Day, Memorial Day, and related events. In 1981 this was changed. The new president broke with older presidents, openly risking the obvious political danger that by identifying with a controversial theological position he would anger many voters. Yet the risk was taken. And the New Christian Right will remain for the foreseeable future an important feature on the political landscape.

The 1984 Campaign

All of this came to a head in the presidential campaign of 1984, the incumbent president and George Bush opposing former vice-president Walter Mondale and congresswoman Geraldine Ferraro. In the estimate of some observers (including myself) the interplay of politics and religion in that campaign was so strong and so profound as to present to Americans "a new agenda" for how we should in the future relate these parts of our public lives.[14]

To summarize the issues, we identify five new developments:

1. An ordained black minister was a major candidate for the presidency.

2. Many Protestant congregations served as places for voter registration and issue education.

3. A woman, explicitly a Roman Catholic and a feminist, achieved a place on a national ticket.

4. The largest denomination in America, the Roman Catholic church, in essence through several

high-ranking leaders instructed its members on how to vote.

5. The presidential candidates themselves carried on an intense if short-lived debate over the American mix of religion and politics.

It is possible in the flux of time that some of these items in the future may fade from the voters' highest priorities. Yet, at this time, it seems fair to say that we have, after the 1984 campaign, a deepening crisis on what it means to be religious in America, and the best efforts of the churches will be needed to help us find our way through its complexities.

We will now explore in greater detail why these five developments have created "a new agenda."

First, Jesse Jackson was the first seminary trained, ordained minister to be a leading candidate for the Oval Office. That in itself was a major break-through. Add to that the fact that his identification as a black was with, in his words, "the desperate, the damned, the disinherited, the disrespected, and the despised," under his "Rainbow Coalition" of all minority groups and tribes "to affirm the oneness of humanity created by God in God's image."[15] Something new indeed had appeared under the sun.

Religion and politics blended in a second way in 1984 as several hundred evangelical and fundamentalist congregations opened their doors to what had been a responsibility of the secular state—the registration of new voters. Congregations were brought directly into a vital part of the electoral process. Most of the leadership came from the New Christian Right under the banner of a letterhead organization, "Americans Concerned for Traditional Values"

(ACTV). Endorsed by President Reagan, its directors included most of the celebrity preachers of the day: Jimmy Swaggart, Rex Humbard, Jim and Tammy Faye Bakker, Jerry Falwell, James Robison, and Kenneth Copeland, among others. Some 100,000 mailings were sent out, and the registration and education programs of ACTV were headed up by eight national field directors working in 25 targeted states. The most popular procedure was to show citizens they could pick up registration forms in church, fill them out when seated in the pews, and drop them in the collection plate. A substantial amount of the money for the program came from Unification Church sources.[16]

The third new development, the candidacy of Geraldine Ferraro, was less directly connected to the new agenda. Yet it did raise new questions, because some Christians opposed having any woman serve so high an office. Others thought she was being anti-Christian because of her support for the Equal Rights Amendment and the pro-choice option on abortion. They were among the many voters who did not want to see the agenda rewritten to include a woman. Yet that agenda was changed, as President Reagan acknowledged when he said, "There will soon be a woman president of the United States, and she will be a Republican." The old American recipe of how religion and politics should mix would hereafter have to come to terms with the likes of Ms. Ferraro.

The fourth issue, that of Roman Catholic involvement in the elective processes, reached the front pages quickly because of the Ferraro stand on abortion. The dispute arose over whether a Roman Catholic lay person holding elective public office could in good conscience approve existing government policy that allowed for legal abortions. Since abortions were contrary to Catholic teaching, then mustn't all Catholics work for their prevention? If Catholics supported abortions, weren't they being poor Catholics? Finally, since these officials needed to face the voters to stay in their positions, then shouldn't the official Catholic position be to oppose their reelection?

But the Catholic church also remembered the centuries of open hostility by Protestants to candidates of their church for public office. They had thought that with the election of Senator John F. Kennedy to the presidency that non-Catholic Americans would recognize that a loyal Catholic could also be a loyal American. Between those two positions emerged the religion/politics issue among Catholics in 1984. So strong, apparently, were Catholic feelings about abortion that they led to the placing of a new item on the agenda. Two archbishops, John J. O'Connor of New York and Bernard Law of Boston, spoke out, urging Catholic citizens to think of their religious convictions as they voted.[17] To some observers that sounded as though church leaders were telling their parishioners how they must vote. One dissenter, columnist Ellen Goodman, responded, "Archbishop Law protests, 'I don't want to be a political boss.' But if a clergyman talks like a political boss and walks like a political boss, he must be judged like a political boss."[18]

What attracted the greatest public attention was the debate between Mondale and Reagan over the proper mix of religion and politics. Shortly after his

renomination, President Reagan at a prayer break-
fast said:

> The truth is, politics and morality are inseparable.
> And as morality's foundation is religion, religion and
> politics are necessarily related. We need religion as
> a guide. We need it because we are imperfect. And
> our government needs the church because only those
> humble enough to admit they're sinners can bring to
> democracy the tolerance it requires in order to sur-
> vive.[19]

That statement touched off a vigorous barrage of
critical editorials and anti-Reagan rallies across the
country. Writers warned of dangerous, divisive, mixing of religion and politics.

Candidate Mondale replied within a few days:

> I believe in an America where all the people have the
> right to pursue their faith not just freely, but also
> without insult or embarrassment; where religious
> freedom is not a passive tolerance, but an active cel-
> ebration of our pluralism. There is no more uplifting
> power on earth than a religious faith which cannot
> be coerced and is tolerant of other beliefs. To coerce
> it is to doubt the sturdiness of our faith. To tell the
> state to enforce the religious life of our people is to
> betray a telling cynicism about the American people.
>
> Moreover, history teaches us that if that force is
> unleashed it will corrupt our faith, divide our nation,
> and embitter our people. No President should attempt
> to transform policy debates into theological disputes.
> He must not let it be thought that political dissent
> from him is un-Christian. And he must not cast op-
> position to his programs as opposition to America.[20]

Then, surprisingly, the issue fell off rapidly as a major dispute. It surfaced only briefly during their first nationally televised debate, and attracted only little attention. President Reagan stirred up a minor fuss when he publicly remarked about the possible approach of the end of the world through the Battle of Armageddon. His remark soon became one more media event.

The *pragmatic* question is this: Did this debate really change any votes? Since winning votes is what campaigning is all about, did the debate make any difference? The best answer seems to be, "very little, if any."[21] But beyond that, the debate, as well as the other four items of the agenda discussed in this chapter, indicates that Americans do recognize the importance of the politics/religion issue but have failed to find any workable resolution to it.

What stands out from the 1984 election is that first, the old ways of understanding American politics as being bloc voting (farm vote, Jewish vote, labor union vote, or solid South vote) is past. The voters in their tribes are motivated by other sources.

Second, Americans are extremely puzzled and divided over how religion and politics should blend. They seem to recognize that the older recipe, the one that had existed before President Reagan's contribution, has disappeared, but they wonder what will take its place. Will the New Christian Right, and the opposition from mainstream American Christianity which it provokes, demand a larger voice in forming public policy? Is the potential candidacy of TV celebrity Pat Robertson for the presidency in 1988 proof of that? So, in a time of deepening crisis, what should the churches be doing to meet the needs of their people and those of the citizens at large?

What Is at Stake?

What have we decided so far in this chapter? That we cannot avoid being political about our faith; that when we face difficult religious or moral decisions, we see them more through the eyes of our personal priorities than that of institutions such as the churches; that despite all this, we still look to the churches for guidance and inspiration; and that the churches, in fulfilling their appointed mission on this earth, are at their best when such guidance is forthcoming.

In his recent survey of American church life, George Gallup discovered "we are in a period of enormous opportunity for the churches of this nation," one in which the churches should "take a very practical 'how to' approach to America's spiritual needs."[22] He wrote that people need to "understand what it means to be a disciple, how religious commitment can be deepened, how to live out one's faith. . . . We want our religious faith to deepen. It is up to the churches to tell us how to do this."

That is what is at stake for the churches. And when we talk of the "church" we recognize that it has different levels of ministry. At the headquarters level, where the vast expert resources of a denomination are available, churches need to continue and improve the development of social statements. Just as the crises they address continue to worsen, so the national voice should continue to be "more vivid, intelligible, incisive, persuasive, rooted in biblical and theological sources."[23] Nothing is quite so helpful as the insight of a specialist whose teaching is specific and to the point.

At the same time such statements should avoid using polemical, politically partisan language, and speaking on too many issues. Too long a list trivializes such statements and cheapens the prophetic voice of moral authority within the church. In a broader sense, as James Reichley of the Brookings Institution reminds us, church statements serve a wide public function: "From the standpoint of the public good, the most important service churches offer to secular life in a free society is the nurturing of moral values that help humanize capitalism and give direction to a democracy."[24]

The difficulty arises when church leaders must decide the issues on which to speak. Clearly those such as civil rights or nuclear war or abortion are fundamentally *moral* and call out for the church's voice. But our public policy makers work with a host of other issues as well, such as *administrative* reforms that are technical or pragmatic. For the church to speak on such technical issues would turn it into a pleader for special causes. To know the difference between these two kinds of issues is exceedingly difficult, but exceedingly important. Perhaps the best advice here is that of Richard John Neuhaus: "The church is nothing less than the bride of Christ. It should be neither of the left nor of the right nor of the spineless middle. We must work towards the time when people don't have to feel they must choose their church on the basis of its politics."[25]

The local congregation offers the best opportunity for the church to be a "how to" problem solver, as called for by Gallup. There, the statements from the national office can be worked through within as much time and detail as interest permits. Too often (from my experience) parishes have avoided direct explorations of the highly controversial issues because of the strong feelings these generate. At that point, leaders need to remind us of the mission of the church to the world, of the frailty but necessity of human insights, and that the *unity* of being one in the body does not mean *uniformity*.

Even more concretely, local parishes should provide more "channels of support and action for its laity." Two Lutheran leaders wrote, "We need more groups prepared to act on the basis of the social statements, either the social ministry committee or ad hoc groups created for a specific purpose." Robert Benne and Carl Braaten have reminded us: "a healthy pluralism should be the order of the day."[26] That pluralism is an umbrella reaching over a wide variety of political and economic convictions, and over a wide variety of ministries.

Consider, as an example, some of the expressions of the church's outreach as were carried out in the Twin Cities area of Minnesota on the weekend of October 13, 1985. Churches presented programs on New Testament community "and its healing potential," on evangelism abroad and at home, on assertiveness classes for men, on "What the devil's wrong with rock music?" on "sexual abuse and the teenager," on peacemaking, on small-group experience for women, on religious autobiography, on "South

Africa today," on feminist spirituality, on "growing older meaningfully," and on war and famine.

To sum up, the problem is not so much finding problems to which the churches can speak meaningfully as it is recognizing that the church serves as a central proclaimer of the gospel to our world. For all of its limitations, it has the potential for renewing and uniting our disjointed lives. It does not offer an exhaustive blueprint of answers to every moral issue. Rather, it proclaims the gospel for our nurturing. Its source, the Bible, is not a political handbook, but the good news. That good news calls its listeners to heed the words of Charles Colson: "He who would lead, let him serve. That admonition is radically opposed to the self-aggrandizing nature of American politics. For the Christian, the goal in politics is not power, but justice."[27]

Finally, then, what is justice? Steven V. Monsma has suggested it is protecting that which is necessary or helpful in order for people to live the joyful, creative, loving lives God intends for his children.[28] That would include, in the estimate of Charles Lutz, facing the issues of resolving human conflict without resort to lethal force, insisting on justice "in relationships among even sinful human beings," caring for the hungry and the poor, and ensuring that the resources of the entire earth are used for all the people of the earth.[29]

So we return to the beginning. Being religious in America grows increasingly complex. Alone, or in our own tribes, each of us faces insurmountable barriers to being effective witnesses. But as people of faith, we can choose to get involved. We have the resources to face this crisis. We have only to use them.

Discussion Questions

1. Do you think the churches should offer opportunities for study and investigation such as those in the trip to Central America described in this chapter?
2. By ministering to the spiritual side of the believer, does the church in effect also minister directly to the social side? Is there truth in that old adage "Let there be peace on earth and let it begin with me?"
3. What did you like or not like about the mixing of religion and politics in the 1984 presidential campaign?
4. Should any special restrictions apply to having an ordained minister run for the presidency?
5. How closely do you look at the religious faith of a candidate?
6. Do you agree with Peter Berger, noted scholar and Lutheran lay leader, who said, "Why don't the churches just shut up?" (*Christian Science Monitor*, October 18, 1985, p. 85).
7. Assume you were on the education board of your local congregation. A parishioner tells your group there are too many social justice and political items on your agenda for the upcoming year. He or she asks you to "stick to the gospel." What would be your reply?

CHAPTER SIX

Religion and the Public Schools: The Crisis for America's Future

Of the tribal conflicts which are shaping our crises today, none has created more anguish and clamor than those about the public schools. The struggles there are so far-reaching and numerous as to defy simple analysis. This chapter explores some of those still in sharp dispute. By way of introducing their complexity, we look first at one that *seems* to have been settled, but for reasons which we will consider below, is still another of the deepening crises. That is the issue of the singing of Christmas carols and hymns in public schools.

For over a decade now, communities, churches, school leaders, and students across the nation have been locked in an often bitter dispute over whether a violation of the separation of church and state occurs when Christmas music is performed at the schools. Do carols constitute an "establishment of religion" because they are done on public property, paid

97

for by tax dollars? Do they not resonate with explicitly Christian doctrine and teaching, thus serving as a worship service for a captive audience?

This issue is so important that it became the source of major litigation, finally reaching the Supreme Court. The Court ruled in *Flory* v. *Sioux Falls School District* (449 U.S.987). The guidelines which that district had established were upheld by lower appeal courts, and the highest tribunal affirmed those by refusing to review the rulings. The guidelines stated:

1. Holidays which have a religious and a secular basis may be observed in the public schools.

2. The historical and contemporary values and the origin of religious holidays may be explained in an unbiased and objective manner without sectarian indoctrination.

3. Music, art, literature and drama having religious themes or basis are permitted . . . if presented in a prudent and objective manner and as a traditional part of the cultural and religious heritage of the particular holiday.

4. The use of religious symbols such as a cross, menorah, crescent, Star of David, creche, symbols of Native American religions or other symbols that are part of a religious holiday is permitted as a teaching aid or resource. . . . Among these holidays are included Christmas, Easter, Passover, Hanukkah, St. Valentine's Day, St. Patrick's Day, Thanksgiving and Halloween.[1]

But in the last few years some parents and taxpayers have continued to press for eliminating such practices. They argue that such observances are the opening wedge to introduce sectarian religion into the public schools. In some cities, such as Rochester,

Minnesota, they made their case the basis of the candidacies for election to the public school board. Voters understood that from such disputes some potentially expensive lawsuits could emerge that might cost the taxpayers considerable money, none of which would go for educational programs. So, since carols were undeniably a source of community conflict, why not just eliminate them? Why try to solve an unsolvable problem?

Here a religious issue worked its way into partisan politicking. The results have often resulted in sharp acrimony among voters, parents, teachers, administrators, and students over the extent to which some kind of religious expression of the Christmas holiday season should be allowed in public institutions. Despite the "Sioux Falls Guidelines," some districts remained locked in disputation.

The Larger Issues

This crisis is intensive because, for most of American history, such issues would not have emerged at all or would have been settled on the local level. Until well into the 20th century, expressions of evangelical and mainline Protestantism, such as singing carols, were considered appropriate in such public institutions as the schools. In our day, however, the increasingly diverse ethnic and tribal character of the American populace has contributed to growing concern over religious observances in tax-supported institutions. An increasing number of minority groups protect their interests by using lawsuits against majority practices. This has created very wide differences over what the tax-supported public schools should be doing about religion. The schools have become battlegrounds (the word is not too strong) for competing armies who have chosen to make their stand for their cause here and now. That amounts to a triple crisis.

First, Americans have benefited greatly from these public schools, surely one of our great contributions to world civilization. They have stood, in the words of Supreme Court Justice Felix Frankfurter, as "at once the symbol of our democracy and the most pervasive means of promoting our common destiny." America's future rests greatly on the extent to which its schools can continue to fulfill that mission. *How can we protect that in our increasingly tribalistic warfare?*

Second, the crisis revolves around a clear religious issue, one central to the American expression of religious pluralism. We expect our schools to symbolize and enrich our democracy and promote our common destiny. We have decided that one major way to achieve that is to keep church and state in their respective spheres. I have already said that the test of a truly democratic society is found in how it protects its dissenters and its diversity. In the United States diversity and respect for the rights of minorities are synonymous with our religious pluralism. We recognize that our civic and public institutions are indispensable in protecting this pluralism. And one major public institution to instill this cherished commitment is the public school. *But what should the schools do about religion?*

Third, in the 1980s, critics of the public schools have invented a new theory as to why the schools seem to fall short of their mission. This is the idea that a planned conspiracy, an organized plot by proponents of *secular humanism,* has arisen to take over the schools—and the rest of American public life—to suit its own distorted purposes. No longer, as in past American history, does the conspiracy come from Roman Catholics or Jews or British bankers or those "soft on communism"—all popular conspiratorial interpretations of our past. Now it is from "secular humanists." *What is their case, and how does it affect the crisis we face?*

What Is the Problem?

These are the issues we will consider in this chapter. They are interrelated, and we will look at them that way. Before we look for answers to these issues we need first to look in some detail at what the dilemma is all about. Most critics of the schools agree in varying degrees to this summary:

1. The schools are failing in their responsibilities to teach the three R's.

2. The schools have become near jungles of disorder, lacking any semblance of discipline and respect.

3. Teachers are more concerned with salaries, fringe benefits, and obtaining power, usually through unions, than in teaching the young.

4. Those who are best qualified to shape policy for children—parents—are ignored.

5. Whatever it is the schools are trying to do about moral and religious concerns is failing.[2]

That last judgment involves our concerns in this book. We can restate the issue this way: (1) everyone wants some form of instruction in religion and morality in the public schools; (2) everyone believes their own agenda of morality and religious instruction is the best one for the public schools; (3) everyone believes pluralism and good will are necessary in working out problems of curriculum and other school activities; (4) everyone believes they themselves have gone as far as they can to accommodate their principles with those with whom they disagree; (5) everyone knows that in such excruciating dilemmas, the American people have accepted the Supreme Court as the final arbiter of cases in dispute.

The Supreme Court has, indeed, taken on that responsibility. This is known as the "secular regulation" rule. This distinguishes between religious beliefs and religious actions:

> Religious beliefs admittedly must have absolute protection, but actions, even though purporting to be taken for religious reasons or as part of religious observances, must conform with the regulations established by the community to protect public order, health, welfare, and morals.[3]

On this basis the Supreme Court has rejected a variety of religious practices, such as polygamy, snake handling, refusals on blood transfusions, and control over juvenile behavior.

Putting it another way, the Supreme Court has attempted to remain *neutral* among the many interest groups seeking to influence religious and moral expressions in the public schools. This neutrality harmonizes well with the convictions of those seekers who in the late 1960s chose to expand or redefine their understanding of religion. For them faith was now more personal, intuitive, and experiential. They thought that no consensual definition of "religious faith" could or should be made operative for our society. Hence, these believers contended, the public schools should make every effort to offer academically sound, value-free, neutral presentations of religious and ethical subjects. Furthermore, no religious practice of observance should be allowed within these institutions, which are paid for by public revenues.

In its landmark decisions of 1962 and 1963 the Supreme Court disallowed any organized expression of prayer or Bible reading. It allowed the teaching of courses in religion, but stated the schools must be neutral; that is, they must avoid institutional or sectarian practices. To this date it has adhered to that interpretation of the "establishment" and "free exercise" clauses of the First Amendment. However, in late 1985, high-ranking administration officials (including the attorney general and the secretary of education) argued that those Court decisions "took God out of the schools."

Martin E. Marty has reminded us, however, that the Court did no such thing. He pointed out that "many of the politically popular calls to 'put God back into the schools' by allowing devotional services come from the Midwest and West, where in 1962 74.05 percent, and 91.38 percent, respectively, of the schools did *not* have such practices'. . . . The people 'took God out,' if God was out."[4]

But to such reasoning a substantial number of Americans reply that there is no such thing as neutrality. To them, when a school district or a court rules out any overt religious practice (such as carols or school prayers), they are in fact being antireligious. If a court rules against, say, the teaching of creationism in biology classes in the name of neutrality, it is endorsing a religious position—that God was absent during the creation of life in this universe. That argument, in turn, has produced its critics, which suggests that while everyone agrees we should keep pluralism alive in our schools, no one is willing to compromise with their adversaries.

The Case of Secular Humanism

Interpreters of American history have often claimed that there were well-organized conspiratorial groups seeking the overthrow of the government. Believers in conspiracies insist that once exposed, these conspirators will disappear and God will again rule among his covenanted people. Well-known examples of such plots are the anti-Catholic movements of the 1840s, the anti-Jewish activities of the 1920s, and the charge in the 1960s that communism had taken over American Protestantism.[5]

In our day, the activist New Christian Right claims that secular humanism is destroying our educational system. They use the term *secular humanism* to mean that "man is the measure of all things." They also believe that whatever steps are necessary to remove such subversive people must be taken by God-fearing Christians. Believers in this conspiracy find their enemy everywhere: in the media, the churches, education, government, entertainment, labor unions, the American Civil Liberties Union, the National Education Association, the National Organization of Women, the National Association for the Advancement of Colored People—to name a few. They charge that some 275,000 such anti-God people permeate all of American life. The critics charge that the humanists reject "any supernatural conception of the universe and affirm that ethical values are human and have no meaning independent of human experience." To the New Christian Right, these secular humanists are not simply ivory-tower academics, but are the leaders for abortion, free use of drugs, liberalized gambling, prostitution, and other "evils."[6] Unless the power of these secular humanists is destroyed—in the schools and elsewhere—America will be destroyed.

The Hatch Amendment

If the indictment by New Christian Right was simply good political polemics, aimed at raising funds and building support, it might not attract our attention here. But it has been written into the statute books of U.S. law in the form of the Hatch Amendment, named for its sponsor Senator Orrin G. Hatch, a republican senator from Utah.

During the election-minded months of 1984 the Senate, following the lead of the House, passed by an 86–3 margin a bill (the "Education for Economic Security Act") authorizing some 75 million dollars for improving schools (named "magnet schools") in communities experiencing racial desegregation problems. To this Hatch added, "Grants under this title may not be used for consultants, for transportation, or for any activity which does not augment improvement, or for courses of instruction the substance of which is secular humanism."[7] New Christian Right groups added that clause to another Senator Hatch amendment, this of 1978, which required schools to obtain parental permission before giving pupils psychological tests. This was intended to prevent the humanists from using children for guinea pig tests or other forms of "mind-bending brainwashing."[8]

Even though the Senate, Senator Hatch, and the Department of Education could not agree on a definition of *secular humanism,* some Rightist groups moved to use the term to purge such alleged influences from the schools. For instance, the movie *Romeo and Juliet* was removed from a Missouri high school, citing the Hatch Amendment. In Georgia a school superintendent told his district teachers to restrict discussion of sex education, teenage suicide, evolution, communism, and "valuing." In Texas a high school teacher told the *New York Times,* "I think twice about what I'm doing here. Is there anything controversial in the lesson plan? If there is, I won't use it. I won't use things where a kid has to make a judgment."[9] In brief, the public schools have been turned for some into a battleground over morality and religion.

Four Such Battlegrounds

In the mid-1980s we can discern at least four such areas of warfare: voluntary school prayer, equal access, creationism, and the moment of silence. All of these issues are still very much alive today and most likely will be for the foreseeable future. Each case has its own characteristics, but the four share at least this much in common: each contains a freedom *for* and a freedom *from* argument. Those who claim that America was and still is a Christian nation want to keep the public schools free for advancing their faith, and free from the influence of the secular humanists. But those who hold that ours is a secular state insist that Americans must be free to pursue religious freedom for themselves in their own manner and free from their perceived enemies, the New Christian Rightists who seek to impose uniformity.

School Prayer

The most widely publicized and bitterly fought battle centers on voluntary school prayer. The constitutional amendment proposed in 1984 reads:

(1) Nothing in this Constitution shall be construed to prohibit individual or group prayer in public schools or other public institutions. (2) No person shall be required by the United States or any state to participate in prayer. (3) Nor shall the United States or any state compose the words of any prayer to be said in the public schools.

A careful student of the issue, Phillip E. Hammond, pointed out that the second sentence "has long been recognized as the law of the land." The third has explicitly been law since 1962 with the ban on the New York Regent's prayer in *Engle* v. *Vitale*. That leaves the first sentence. Hammond asks: "What does it make legal that is now illegal? The answer is: Nothing."[10] Then, we may ask, what did the amendment's supporters hope to achieve? When we cut through the torrents of rhetoric flooding the debate, we find they want a constitutionally endorsed expression of government support for the place of prayer and faith in the public schools. They want a public witness that America is a religious nation.

But why specifically in the public school? The supporters of the amendment believe the secular humanists have taken control there and by so doing have set America on a course of destruction. Furthermore, for many Americans the current declining status of these schools has come to symbolize their own lack of control over decisions that directly influence their lives. For many, in this age of bewildering social change, the school stood as the center for family, for neighborhood, for grass roots, and for personal participation in public policy making. To deny children the right to pray meant a rejection of the belief that America was unique.

During the fervid rallies of March 1984, on Capitol Hill, one supporter carried a sign "Return God to Our Schools. And Live as a Nation under Christ." Other citizens launched a "Save Our Schools Crusade," featuring school prayer as the indispensible means to restore order and curb violence, to eliminate drug and alcohol abuse, illegitimate births, and vandalism.[11]

That was a tall order for prayer, too tall, in fact, for other religious groups who throughout the years of battle had vigorously opposed this amendment. The United States senators who were to vote on the proposal knew from long and fervent lobbying that

Roman Catholics, Episcopalians, Lutherans, Presbyterians, the United Church of Christ, several Baptist groups, and others stood adamantly against the measure. They knew that certain religious activities had long been and continued to be available to the students. These included individual silent prayer at any time or place; a vocal prayer by a student, so long as the prayers did not interrupt the educational process or infringe on the religious liberty of other students; giving thanks for meals silently or vocally, so long as the prayer was student-initiated and not school sponsored; carrying Bibles and using them for devotional reading, so long as that did not interfere with classroom work; student discussion of religious views with classmates, not dependent upon school endorsement or outside proselytization; and off-campus religious instruction provided by school boards.[12]

In the final vote, the amendment lost 56-44, 11 votes short of the two-thirds needed for ratification. Despite warnings from proponents that any dissenting senator would face the wrath of voters in November 1984, the 44 senators voted as they had originally indicated. President Reagan's warning in August of that year that the opponents were themselves "intolerant of religion" failed to win additional votes. In turn, those senators voting against the school-prayer amendment were saying that religious education and involvement should continue to flourish voluntarily in church, synagogue, and home.

The battle goes on, and the "Save Our Schools Crusade" has recently announced plans for a new offensive.

Equal Access

A proposal known as "equal access" emerged as one alternative to prayer and as a guarantee that students could in a constitutional way discuss religious subjects on school property. Its sponsors had learned that since 1982 many school administrators believed they must prohibit any religiously oriented activity by students at any time on school premises. A substantial number of political and religious leaders, from all along the ideological spectrum, concluded that such prohibitions infringed on the rights of free speech, free association, and free exercise of religion. Why shouldn't students be able to discuss religious subjects when in school, just like those who were pursuing chess or stamp collecting or similar extracurricular activities?

The momentum for an equal access bill appeared in 1982, supported by a wide variety of religious groups, but opposed by several civil libertarian organizations. The latter feared the bill would give preferred status to speech with a religious content, because no other activity was so protected. They thought that teachers or nonschool organizations (such as cults) might inject themselves into the student discussions. To meet such criticism, the proponents drew up general guidelines, which were attached to the bill. It became law in August 1985, with the clear stipulation that the students needed local protection. A good example of that is in the guidelines drawn up for John Marshall Senior High School, Rochester, Minnesota:

Nonschool persons may not initiate, direct, conduct,

or regularly attend such meetings; and school employees or agents shall not participate or be present at such meetings except for custodial purposes.

Both sides knew the law would be taken into the courts. This was done in several states, the most important test case to reach the Supreme Court being from Williamsport, Pennsylvania. Whatever the decision of that tribunal, equal access indicates again how far apart Americans stand from each other in resolving issues of religion in the schools.[13]

Support for equal access came quickly and strongly from a wide segment of the populace. What stands out clearly is that Americans want to believe that the public schools can and should be one place where being religious and obeying the Constitution are possible *at the same time*. Despite the heated claims during the mid-1980s that schools were being destroyed by atheists, that the Senate was hostile to children's prayers, or that many religious bodies were soft on secularism, the zealous support for equal access suggests that Americans recognize the importance of voluntary participation in public expressions of faith.

The Teaching of Creationism

Both prayer and equal access are procedural freedoms; they avoid any involvement with school curricula. While they were being discussed, however, a bitter debate over curriculum crowded into the public arena. This battle revolves around what is known as "scientific creationism." The battle is not over whether the account of creation in Genesis is accepted to be taught in the public school. According to James E. Wood Jr., it "is clearly permissible and has never been seriously questioned in the courts."[14] Rather, the struggle rotates around the demands by anti-evolutionists that creationism be taught as science and be granted equal time with evolutionist thought. According to these antievolutionists, creationism is scientifically sound as well as consistent with their religious understanding of God's activity in the natural world. Hence, the creationists would introduce a theological conviction into the public school curriculum as science.[15]

To give creationists equal time would obviously mean that the government (in this case, the schools) would be endorsing a theological doctrine. That was clearly objectionable to many of the scientific community. On a practical level, its implementation would mean the public schools would now have to make time and resources available, not only for creationism, but for the teaching of any sectarian doctrine.[16]

On that basis, the landmark decision in 1982 by Judge William Overton, which declared unconstitutional an Arkansas creationism law, has virtually ended any further discussion of this issue. But for the creationists the issue goes beyond the scientific integrity of evolution. The fact that evolution has stood up under repeated court tests indicates to them how far America has chosen to believe secular humanism rather than the Word of God. According to their interpretation, America was a great and good society, honoring God until evolution (along with higher criticism of the Bible) came along to shake the foundations. They see evolution as teaching that this universe is an accident without divine order or higher law. And with equal fervor the scientific community, along with many religious organizations and civil libertarian groups, rejects creationism as nothing but doctrinal proselytizing in the public schools. The battle continues.

Moment of Silence

After the Supreme Court had declared unconstitutional any organized public school prayers, certain leaders and school districts attempted to replace those prayers with one or more alternatives. This idea took hold in several states; by the mid-1980s 23 states had such provisions, usually providing a minute of silence at the beginning of the school day for students to engage in "contemplation or introspection." Several of these programs had been challenged in the lower courts as violating the Supreme Court ban on prayers. Some states recast their laws to provide for simple meditation or reflection. But critics concluded these were but rationalizations for allowing some form of scheduled prayer. In reply, the proponents argued these were voluntary, silent, and totally personal. What could be the harm in that?[18]

Some did see harm and pressed for disallowance. In June 1985, in a very carefully worded ruling, the Supreme Court disallowed moments of silence that were announced or intended to serve as opportunities for prayer. If the moment were only for meditation or a secular purpose, then such practice could be allowed.

The whole controversy is instructive for several reasons. First, it underlines how complex and unpredictable are Supreme Court rulings on church/ state cases regarding religion in the public school; second, how determined the Justices are to maintain their decisions of 1962 and 1963 to keep organized religious observances out of the public schools; third, how sure we can be that the proponents of school prayer will continue to press their case; fourth, the likelihood that constitutional amendments to allow moments of silence in public schools will probably fail to attract strong public support.

What Is the Message?

Most Americans seem to want an opportunity to express religious faith in the public schools, but it should be voluntary, and guidelines should be flexible and sensitive to local concerns. In other words, America is not ready to follow the New Christian Right in "returning this nation to God," or any such crusade. That is too objectionable and frightening to the rank and file of voters. That is not the way Americans want to be religious. Yet some broadly worded provisions for equal access or a moment of silence seem to attract considerable support.

In short, Americans are not ready to abandon the public schools; only some 10% of the of the total eligible population of children are attending one of the variety of religious and secular alternative school systems. This means that the responsibility for instructing children "in the fear and the admonition of the Lord" is still reserved for the home, the synagogue, and the church.

What Is at Stake?

First, the battle is not simply one between the New Christian Right and the public schools. If it were just that, the agenda for reform would be more precise. Instead, the issues are exceedingly complex. Workable solutions require a long-term commitment, a willingness to keep fully informed, and the belief that those with whom we may disagree share our zeal for upgrading public education. What is at stake is the integrity and academic freedom of the public schools against those who promote a more restricted and sectarian outlook.

In other words, some profound but easily overlooked values are at stake. The public schools should continue to protect students from discrimination on the basis of sex, race, national origins, *and* religion. The schools are not churches, and to the consternation of those who want them to be so, vocal and energetic minorities are pressing the majority to respect every tradition represented within school walls. Otherwise, as Martin E. Marty has suggested, an amendment to restore religious exercises in the public schools would create havoc.

Let them have it. Let mainline Methodists, for example, find that their children come home "voluntarily" shaped by aggressive fundamentalists, or fundamentalists' kids find themselves outnumbered by liberals. Let the PTA be the adjudicating body over disputes, the school board the liturgist, the voting booth the determiner of prayer-book revision—and the psychologist the handler of the outsider kids who, in conscience, don't want someone else to do their praying for them. Who will discipline the public teacher? Who will punish the undisciplined teacher?[19]

Second, by allowing or not interfering in the public schools' determination to protect the rights of all, we are affirming the goodness of everyone's religious conviction and celebrating the integrity of freedom of conscience in issues of belief and commitment. Such a commitment reminds us of the diversity of God's creation.

Third, we must keep alert to simplistic, moralistic, emotional explanations of what ails our schools. There is no conspiracy by any group to destroy the schools. There are no perverted instructors seeking to destroy student morals with programs such as "values clarification." There are no traitors to Americanism bent on creating enemies of the state. There are many teachers who seek to protect the religious freedom of everyone by seeing that the freedom of each minority is protected. That is an attitude we need to affirm.

Beyond such affirmations, what can be done? We can follow legislative proposals at all levels of government that would affect the schools. For example, is the Hatch Amendment about the teaching of secular humanism being enforced in your district? Next, we can cooperate with other like-minded groups and individuals who share our values. As early as 1787 James Madison understood that American democracy worked best when it encouraged the participation of special interest groups (he called them "factions") in hammering out social policy. We can

encourage the teaching about religion through courses in literature, history, and social studies. We can
encourage the efforts of those teachers who demon-
strate the nobility of vision that is essential for a
dedicated, informed citizenry.

Discussion Questions

1. What first-hand knowledge do you have about
   how well the public schools are doing?
2. Why are conspiracy interpretations so popular?
   Why do they continue to reoccur?
3. Is there a difference between a "secular state" (as
   discussed on p. 87) and the "humanistic state" as
   defined by the New Christian Right today?
4. Have your views changed over the years on voluntary school prayer or creationism? Why do people find it so hard to compromise on these issues?
5. How can parents and church members help public
   school teachers?

CHAPTER SEVEN

Faithful to What We Believe

We want to be religious in America. But are we religious *because* we are Americans or *in spite of* our being Americans? Does living in this particular nation make any particular difference for our faith? In this concluding chapter we attempt to answer those questions. In doing so, we recognize that the most cherished dimensions of our faith transcend national loyalties. We also acknowledge that among people who cherish religious freedom, we will find other valid answers to these questions.

Being religious is not totally an individualistic matter; it is more than a do-your-own thing enterprise. As we have already seen in this book, certain traditions, values, and customs do flourish here, as in every nation. These together help create a quality we refer to as "American." We have specific constitutional protections, certain historical patterns of immigration, certain prevailing social and economic

119

divisions among us that are uniquely ours. So, while one's inner religious life does transcend national boundaries, our public expressions take on a uniquely national configuration.

We can understand that quality from at least two viewpoints. First, religious faith (which in America means the Judeo-Christian tradition) cannot be placed into any single pigeonhole. Faith has both an inner and an outer history; it is both spirit and body, both a past and a present. It is like a many-sided diamond. Hence as Samuel S. Hill Jr. said about Christianity, it "should prize search, quest, movement, dialectic, paradox, mystery, irony and humor, as well as certainty and boldness of conviction and earnestness of spirit."[1] All of these qualities are included in being religious.

Secondly, many believers know that being religious is primarily a participation in the organized communities of faith—churches and synagogues. That involvement is central to their expression of faith. The church supports, admonishes, directs, and nourishes their faith. In large groups they can carry out social ministries that are beyond the reach of individuals or the local congregation. Churches serve as loving communities, as sources of creative good will. Being religious embraces the human quality of needing help and giving help.

Yet for untold numbers of believers the church seems obsolete, a remnant from the past that they have outgrown. Theirs is something like the "invisible religion" described in Chapter 2. They think of themselves as religious, but they find any institutional expression of religion unnecessary. So, church involvement stands as one, but not the exclusive, quality of being religious.

Being religious in America involves at least these qualities: being *public,* being *political,* being *pluralistic,* being *prophetic,* and being *persuasive.*

Being Religious Means Being Public

Being religious means to acknowledge the *public* dimension of faith. Robert Bellah and his associates have said it well: "We find ourselves not independently of other people and institutions but through them. We never get to the bottom of our selves on our own. We discover who we are face to face and side by side with others in work, love, and learning."[2]

Being public means running the risk of conflict with other tribal interests. Undoubtedly some religious people keep their faith to themselves to avoid such conflict. Yet accepting conflict in public means we have freedom for experiencing conflicting viewpoints, including religious ones. Our public expressions of faith are less a "doing to" others who disagree with us and more a "being with" our families, friends, and communities.[3]

In this day of high-powered public relations techniques, we need to make one qualification about being public. It does not mean being publicity minded. We can find in certain of Jesus' teachings a priority for keeping information about his ministry within the circle of followers, of keeping prayer away from the street corners, of not doing acts of righteousness before others, of keeping the right hand from knowing what the left hand is doing.[4] Being religious in public does not mean more publicity, depending on the goodness that comes from the interaction with others who also need and offer help.

Being Religious Means Being Political

We have a wide variety of meanings for the word *politics;* we use it to describe what goes on in our business offices, our schools, our churches, and so on. In this book, politics means the process by which we decide public policy, see that our officials respond to it, and hold them accountable for putting it into our public lives. And that means we get involved in politics. Because of our religious interests, we are especially alert to politics as it relates to matters of justice, social welfare, law enforcement, and family protection.

Putting it in another way, we cannot avoid being political. To shun all political activity is to cast a vote for saying we think social-justice issues are not a part of our religious lives—and that in itself is a political statement. For most Americans, being political means keeping informed on the issues, participating informally with friends and colleagues in decision making, and voting. It means applying one's religious and moral convictions as norms and as motivators for political involvement.

Here, of course, we recognize the need to avoid identifying one particular tribal loyalty as *the* will of God. Reinhold Niebuhr reminded us that we are finite and contingent creatures, tending to endow the contingent values of our lives and culture, of our truths and loyalties, with an absolute significance they do not deserve. Only God is the source of such an absolute. Yet faith requires a certain boldness and earnestness; risk taking is essential to public faith.

Does that mean we will come into conflict with friends or colleagues? Should religious faith go out of its way to risk that? Charles Lutz has spoken directly to that concern: "The gospel is God's declaration. Our political behavior is a part of our response to God's activity. The gospel is good news from God. Our social witness involves good advice from the people of God in seeking the public good along with many others. The gospel motivates us. It does not provide us with a blueprint for ordering society."[5] Our tribal loyalties are not the will of God, but we have a responsibility to work for them in the political arena. As the presiding bishop of the American Lutheran Church, David Preus, has stated it, that responsibility comes from the scriptural admonition about serving the cup of cold water, of providing bread for the hungry and freedom for the oppressed, and doing justice, and showing mercy.[6]

Being Religious Means Being Pluralistic

As Americans we respect the great tradition of religious pluralism. That may not be as easy as it sounds. It involves, first, showing respect for the religious traditions and expressions of fellow citizens, and a certain willingness to celebrate those differences. But in our day of heightened tribal loyalties, such celebration seems to be declining. We have seen the results of such decline in the stalemate over the issue of religion in the public schools.

Secondly, being pluralistic means accepting the fact that our society need not be Christianized in order for it to serve the needs of our neighbors. As Paul Sonnack has said, "The church is not meant to compete with society or offer itself as a substitute for it."[7] The church and believers are "to cooperate with society and its power to the extent that love and law serve the same end, viz., the good of the neighbor." With our fierce tribal loyalties today, serving our neighbor seems rather low on the list of social priorities.

Thirdly, being pluralistic means accepting both compromise and conflict as healthy for our public lives. Compromise comes hard for a people of faith who believe they have some insight into that which is eternal and transcendent. But so do others. Nowhere in our day is that more evident, or irritating to many, than in the new controversy over religion mixing with politics as espoused by the New Christian Right. Because that faction seems bent on having its way without compromise towards the larger public, our loyalty to pluralism is being tested. What hopefully will emerge from this dialog is a recognition that our faith is better served when open and— if necessary—divisive conflict is accepted as normal and welcome for the public concerns of the churches.

Being Religious Means Being Prophetic

The word *prophetic* does not mean having the ability to foretell the future. It means being willing to bring to public life a sense of right and wrong, of evaluation and judgment on the quality of that public

life. The word here is used in accord with the prophetic tradition of the Old Testament.

But, as church history reveals, far too often the
churches have muted their prophetic voice. They
have decided that worldly standards of size and numbers and wealth are the criteria for success. James
Wood has reminded us:

> The mission of the church, therefore, is not only to
> preach justice, but to be a force for justice in the world;
> not only to proclaim the principle of freedom in Christ
> but to be free of alliances with power structures that
> would mute its prophetic voice; . . . not only to con-
> demn evil, but to disassociate itself from evil.[8]

Two examples from contemporary ministry programs come to mind. In Cincinnati, Roman Catholic
Father Richard Rohr works to build a prophetic lay
community of believers. Working from the premise
of "Jesus through me" rather than "Jesus for me,"
he helps lead a group of some 250 believers into a
prophetic ministry. "I want to work within the system, but I want to stay as much on the edge as I can.
That's the place of freedom, where you can't be
bought off. I'm just following St. Francis." He told a
reporter, "I always felt I was committed to social
justice. My error was I assumed that once people got
to know Jesus, they'd all be taking care of soup lines
and being against nuclear arms. That didn't happen.
Instead, I was seeing people getting into religion for
religion's sake. Many charismatics were not becoming global universalists; they were just getting into
soft piety again." The reporter concluded, "Soft piety
is not what Richard Rohr has come to bring."[9]

The second is an Episcopalian group, St. Stephen's in San Francisco. It sponsors a number of prayer groups and Bible study groups, and a mostly volunteer team for visiting persons who are sick or homebound. Some in the parish take care of feeding, clothing, and caring for the homeless people and those who are hungry. The church has active social outreach in peace-and-justice programs. The Eucharist is celebrated daily and three times on Sunday, and to the pastor, Father Paul Morrison, that seems to be the empowering source for the members. The parish makes a difference in the life of the community and in the lives of the members. The people there "bring their life, the heart of their life to the communion rail and hold it up and find healing and comfort and walk away somehow renewed, restored and fit for another week in a pretty tough world."[10] Morrison recognizes the prophetic dimension: "The concept that a community can set standards, adopt values, capture conscience, and become authoritative in the life of human beings is not obvious in our culture, and it falls apart without it." St. Stephen's makes that kind of difference.[11]

Being Religious Means Being Persuasive

Being *persuasive* here means using moral persuasion, rather than coercion, to carry the faith into public life. That is more complicated than it may seem at first glance. John Garvey helps us to remember why. Over the centuries, he writes, religious leaders have become "too cozy" with the political powers that be, a situation that inevitably creates abuse within the churches. The identification of a nation's foreign policy with the will of God and the churches' endorsement of that policy is a good example of such coziness.

Garvey makes this point: "A truth which is enforced is not really a truth; a child who parrots the right answers in school without understanding them has learned nothing. Religion at the social level has been that way too often in the past. It betrays its nature and its deepest helpfulness when it is a token of belonging to the crowd of good citizens and respectable people. It may indeed have served well as a social control at certain points in the past, *but that isn't what the prophets or the gospels are about.*"[12]

Nowhere did Jesus attempt to coerce a person into discipleship. His was the power of example, of persuasiveness, of appealing to the best in a person's character, of demonstrating the joys of a life of faith. But can that be done? Might it not be true that ours is an age where power decides what is to be done?

Perhaps, but some concrete ways of being persuasive rather than coercive can tell us what the prophets and the Gospels are all about. Believers can become advocates for public policies consistent with the social witness of our biblical faith. In 1982 the American Lutheran Church outlined such a plan in its call for advocacy. This was defined as:

> group or individual activity seeking to influence societal power centers or processes of decision making, towards *both* justice for those who are relatively voiceless or powerless *and* the well-being of the whole human family, on the basis of an understanding of the biblical vision of community health and wholeness.[13]

Advocacy is not the same thing as lobbying, which can be the pursuit of self-interest legislation. Advocacy is pleading the cause of others or of the whole human family. It is directed at "centers of power, usually economic or political power," but also at the church itself, an institution with considerable power in our society.[14] This may be done by several means: ongoing nurture in our faith and its connections with our societal life, regular preaching of the Word in relation to the needs of the world, promoting social and political dialog among Christians with varying viewpoints, and collective advocacy on a major issue when a consensus among a group of Christians is reached.

The way of persuasion leads to our concluding words. Being voluntary means being willing to see by faith as well as by sight—faith in the promise that beyond the unknowable in this world lies a realm, a love, worthy of our trust. Another way of saying that is, to risk fidelity to a commitment. That commitment means moving out into the world from a specific tradition. One sings for the good of all when it is one's own voice that is heard. One honors God best when the voice of the speaker is authentic.

That authenticity points to the need to remain faithful to what we believe. In our concern for our immediate lives and cares, we dare not forget we are called to be faithful to the kingdom of God. That is our first allegiance. From there, all other responsibilities and loyalties take their direction and find their place among those things which are ultimate. That leads us to see that this kingdom is not political, that it is not the possession of any one nation or people. We are called to do justly, to love mercy, and to walk humbly with God. And we are to do that with all our talents and all our determination, so that ultimately we are faithful to what we believe when we accept the gift of grace and proclaim the gospel.

Americans, with their impressive talents for being up-and-doing problem solvers, have trouble in accepting the gift. Grace, however, is just that, coming from a gracious God. Contrary to humanly created rewards, it is free and unearned. God gives it to us by persuasion, by what he has done and continues to do. Knowing that, when we are being religious, we are responding faithfully to what we believe.

Notes

Chapter 1. Being Religious in America

1. Albert Shulman, *The Religious Heritage of America* (San Diego: A. S. Barnes and Company, 1981), pp. 408.
2. Berrigan, in a symposium, "Does America Still Exist?" *Harper's,* March 1984, pp. 45–46.

Chapter 2. Strange and Troubled Times

1. John Naisbitt, *Megatrends* (New York: Warner Books, 1982), p. 2.
2. Alvin Toffler, *The Third Wave* (New York: William Morrow, 1980), p. 25.
3. Leonard I. Sweet, "The 1960s," in *Evangelicalism and Modern America,* ed. George Marsden (Grand Rapids: Eerdmans, 1984), p. 30.
4. Sydney Ahlstrom, *A Religious History of the American People* (New Haven: Yale University Press, 1972), p. 1079.
5. William McLoughlin, *Revivals, Awakening, and Reform* (Chicago: University of Chicago Press, 1978), pp. xiii, 2.

6. Richard Sennett, *The Fall of Public Man* (New York: Knopf, 1977), p. 259.

7. Robert N. Bellah, et al., *Habits of the Heart: Individualism and Commitment in American Life* (Berkeley: University of California Press, 1985), pp. 101–102; see also Talcott Parsons, "Religion in Postindustrial America," *Social Research* 41 (Summer 1974): 221.

8. Carl Dudley, *Where Have All Our People Gone?* (New York: Pilgrim Press, 1979), pp. 11–12.

9. J. W. Carroll, et al., *Religion in America, 1950 to the Present* (San Francisco: Harper and Row, 1977), p. 25.

10. Joseph H. Fichter, "The Trend to Spiritual Narcissism," *Commonweal,* March 17, 1978, p. 173.

11. Martin E. Marty, "Religion in America since Mid-Century," as cited by Mary Douglas and Steven Tipton, eds., *Religion and America: Spirituality in a Secular Age,* (Boston: Beacon Press, 1983), pp. 283–85.

12. See my *The Politics of Moralism: The New Christian Right in American Life* (Minneapolis: Augsburg, 1981).

Chapter 3. Does God Love America Best?

1. President Reagan as quoted in Larry Rasmussen's "Patriotism Lived: Lessons from Bonhoeffer," *Christianity and Crisis,* June 24, 1985, p. 249.

2. Lance Morrow in *Time,* January 7, 1985, p. 22.

3. Ibid., p. 20.

4. Sydney Ahlstrom, "The American National Faith: Humane, Yet All Too Human," in *Religion and the Humanizing of Man,* ed. James M. Robinson (Waterloo, Canada: Council on the Study of Religion, 1973), p. 109.

5. For Schaeffer, Brown, and Falwell, see Paul Simmons, "Fundamentalism: Courting Civil Religion," Baptist

Joint Committee on Public Affairs, *Report from the Capitol,* September 1981, p. 5.

6. Grant Wacker, "Searching for Norman Rockwell: Popular Evangelicalism in Contemporary America," as quoted in Leonard I. Sweet, ed., *The Evangelical Tradition in America,* (Macon, Ga.: Mercer University Press, 1984), pp. 297 ff.

7. I draw heavily here from James E. Wood Jr., *Nationhood and the Kingdom* (Nashville: Broadman, 1977), pp. 36 ff.

8. Ibid., p. 62.

9. Ibid., pp. 73, 75.

10. Ibid., p. 105.

11. Office of Church and Society, The American Lutheran Church, "The Nature of the Church and Its Relationship with Government," 1979, pp. 3–4; Robert Benne and Carl Braaten, et al., " 'Two Kingdoms' as Social Doctrine," *Dialog,* Summer 1984, pp. 209–10.

12. Ibid., and Paul G. Sonnack, "Two Kingdoms," *Word and World* 4 (Summer 1984): 277.

13. Wilbur Zelinsky, "What It Means When Americans Show the Flag," *Minneapolis Star and Tribune,* July 4, 1985.

14. W. Lloyd Warner, *American Life: Dream and Reality* (Chicago: Phoenix Books, 1962, rev. ed.), p. 8.

15. Mark A. Noll, et al., *The Search for Christian America* (Westchester, Ill.: Crossway, 1983), pp. 130–31.

16. Ibid., p. 134.

17. Paul Simmons, "Fundamentalism: Courting Civil Religion," p. 5

18. Larry Rasmussen, "Patriotism Lived," p. 251.

19. The quote "How Much Is All This Worth?" on pp. 42–43 is from Richard L. Evans' book *May Peace Be with You,* copyright 1960 Harper and Brothers, and is used by permission.

Chapter 4. Pluralism

1. George J. Bryjak and Gary A. May, "The Fall of Sun Myung Moon and the Unification Church in America," *USA Today,* November 1985.

2. Ibid.; David G. Bromley, "Financing the Millennium: The Economic Structure of the Unificationist Movement," *Journal for the Scientific Study of Religion* 24 (September 1985): 253–74; at an SSSR conference in Savannah, Ga., on Oct. 26, 1985, Bromley mentioned the dollar figure used here.

3. Dick Anthony and Thomas Robbins, "Spiritual Innovation and the Crisis of American Civil Religion," as cited by Mary Douglas and Steven Tipton, eds., *Religion and America: Spirituality in a Secular Age* (Boston: Beacon Press, 1983), pp. 234–39.

4. Herbert Richardson, ed., *Constitutional Issues in the Case of Rev. Moon* (New York: Edwin Mellen Press, 1984).

5. Ronald Enroth and J. Gordon Melton, "Why Cults Succeed," *Christianity Today,* March 16, 1984, pp. 15–17; Robert Bellah, et al., *Habits of the Heart* (Berkeley: University of California Press, 1985), pp. 235–37.

6. Enroth and Melton, "Why Cults Succeed," p. 15.

7. Thomas Robbins, "Marginal Movements," *Society,* May/June 1984, p. 48; an excellent discussion is in Rodney Stark and William S. Bainbridge, *The Future of Religion: Secularization, Revival and Cult Formation* (Berkeley: University of California Press, 1985), Chap. 2.

8. Enroth and Melton, "Why Cults Succeed," pp. 16–17.

9. Interview with Walter Martin in *The Arizona State Journal* (Tucson), September 1, 1984, pp. 1G, 3G.

10. Daniel Poling and George Gallup Jr., *The Search for America's Faith* (Nashville: Abingdon, 1980), pp. 17–19.

11. Enroth and Melton, "Why Cults Succeed," pp. 16–17; based also on my conversations with Unificationists; see also Harriet S. Mosatche, *Searching; Practices and Beliefs of the Religious Cults* (New York: Stavron Educational Press, 1983), pp. 371–81.

12. *Minneapolis Star and Tribune,* April 8, 1985; figures are from the Rev. Chung Hwan Kwak of the Unification Church, given at a conference at the Chicago Marriott Hotel, June 29, 1985, which I attended.

13. Saul L. Levine, "Radical Departures," *Psychology Today,* August 1985, p. 23; a good bibliography is Brock Kilbourne and James T. Richardson, "Psychotherapy and New Religions in a Pluralistic Society," *American Psychologist* 39 (March 1984): 237–51.

14. Bromley, "Financing the Millennium," p. 253.

15. Richard Quebedeaux, *New Conversations,* Spring 1982, pp. 11–12; Commission on Faith and Order, National Council of Churches, "A Critique of the Theology of the Unification Church," 1977; news item, *Christian Century,* December 4, 1985, p. 1112.

16. Ibid.; see also the evidence in Herbert Richardson, *Constitutional Issues.*

17. Editorial, *New Yorker,* April 28, 1985, pp. 27–28; *Minneapolis Star and Tribune,* April 8, 1985; *Time,* April 22, 1985, p. 60; *Christianity Today,* April 19, 1985, pp. 50–51; September 7, 1984, pp. 56–62; *Christian Century,* June 5, 1985, p. 577; further documentation on the Unificationists in American politics is in Carolyn Weaver, "Unholy Alliance," *Mother Jones,* January 1986, pp. 14, 16, 17, 44, 46.

18. Tribe's quotation is in the General Baptist Committee on Public Affairs, *Report from the Capitol,* June 1984, p. 8; the most complete documentation is in the Richardson volume, see above, n. 4; *Christian Herald,* October 1984, p. 4; Leo Pfeffer, *Religion, State and the*

Burger Court (Buffalo: Prometheus Books, 1984), pp. 214–15.

19. Baptist Joint Committee, *Report,* June 1984, p. 8; a helpful critical article of Moon is Michael Istkoff, "New Moon," *New Republic,* August 26, 1985, pp. 14–16.

20. Robert Wuthnow, *Experimentation in American Religion* (Princeton: Princeton University Press, 1978), pp. 189–201.

21. Dean M. Kelley, "What Does the Future Hold?" as quoted in Robert McNamara, ed., *Religion: North American Style* (Belmont: Wadsworth Publishing Co., 1984, 2nd ed.), p. 348; see also news story, *Time,* April 22, 1983, p. 60; Thomas Robbins, "Marginal Movements," *Society,* May/June 1984, p. 49.

22. Martin, *Arizona State Journal,* September 1, 1984, pp. 1G, 3G. See also the "anticult" books listed in Donna L'Aline, *The Anti-Cult Movement in America: A Bibliography* (New York: Garland Publishing Co., 1985); Martin E. Marty, "A Special Report," *Christian Century,* July 3–10, 1985, pp. 650–51; ibid., February 14, 1984, pp. 163–65; the definitive study is David G. Bromley and James T. Richardson, eds., *The Brainwashing-Deprogramming Controversy* (New York: Edwin Mellen Press, 1983); see also the best "anti-anti-cult" book, Thomas Robbins, et al., eds., *Cults, Culture, and the Law: Perspectives on New Religious Movements* (Chico, Calif.: Scholars, 1985).

23. A comprehensive guide to such organizations, "Voluntary-Service Opportunities" is in *The Other Side,* January/February 1986, pp. 21–28.

24. J. Gordon Melton and Robert L. Moore, *The Cult Experience* (New York: Pilgrim Press, 1982), p. 106 and Chap. 4.

25. William J. Whalen, "Christians Shouldn't Condemn Cults," *U.S. Catholic,* November 1984, pp. 13–18.

Chapter 5. Public Policy Making and the Churches

1. This section is based on "Point Counter Point," *The Lutheran Standard,* October 4, 1985, pp. 12–16. A helpful follow-up story is in the *Minneapolis Star and Tribune,* December 22, 1985.
2. "Point Counter Point," *The Lutheran Standard,* October 4, 1985, p. 15.
3. Ibid., p. 13.
4. Ibid., p. 39.
5. George Gallup Jr., ed., *Religion in America, 1984* (Princeton: The Gallup Report, 1984), pp. 1–18.
6. Ibid., p. 12; *U.S. News and World Report,* December 9, 1985, pp. 52–58; this is updated for 1985 in *Christian Science Monitor,* December 6, 1985, pp. 1, 26.
7. Steven Tipton in the verbatim account of a conference, *Religion and Political Campaigns* (Cambridge: Harvard University, 1984), p. 35.
8. James E. Wood Jr., *Nationhood and the Kingdom* (Nashville: Broadman, 1977), p. 83.
9. Ibid., p. 85.
10. Ibid., p. 86.
11. Quoted in ibid., p. 87.
12. Walter Rauschenbusch, as quoted in Wood, *Nationhood and the Kingdom.*
13. A statement by the 12th General Convention of the American Lutheran Church, "Human Law and the Conscience of Believers," Minneapolis, ALC Office of Church and Society, 1984, pp. 5–6.
14. Based on my study of Campaign 1984, "Our Faith and Public Life," American Lutheran Church, Office of Church and Society (1985).
15. Manning Marble, "The Rainbow Coalition: Jesse Jackson and the Politics of Ethnicity," *Cross Currents,* Spring 1984, pp. 25–27.

16. *New York Times,* August 17, 1984, p. 10; ibid., September 10, 1984, p. 12; *Minneapolis Star and Tribune,* September 25, 1984.

17. *National Catholic Reporter,* September 21, 1984, p. 16; Law's statements are in the transcript of "The MacNeil-Lehrer News Hour," September 11, 1984, Transcript no. 2337, p. 7.

18. Goodman's column is in *Minneapolis Star and Tribune,* September 11, 1984; see also news story in *Christianity Today,* December 14, 1984, pp. 26–29.

19. *New York Times,* August 24, 1984, p. 11.

20. Ibid., September 8, 1984, pp. 1, 12.

21. *Minneapolis Star and Tribune,* November 15, 1984; "Election Extra," *Newsweek,* November/December 1984, passim; *Time,* November 19, 1984, passim.

22. Gallup, *Religion in America, 1984,* pp. 12, 13, 18.

23. Robert Benne, Carl Braaten, et al., " 'Two Kingdoms' As Social Doctrine," *Dialog,* Summer 1984, pp. 211–12.

24. See James Reichley's new book *Religion in American Public Life* (Washington: The Brookings Institution, 1985); the quotation is from the *Christian Science Monitor Review,* October 18, 1985, p. 16.

25. Richard John Neuhaus as quoted in *Christianity Today,* February 1, 1985, p. 56.

26. Benne and Braaten, "Two Kingdoms," p. 212.

27. Charles Colson as quoted in "My Turn," *Newsweek,* October 8, 1984, p. 10.

28. Steven V. Monsma, *Pursuing Justice in a Sinful World* (Grand Rapids: Eerdmans, 1984), pp. 338–39.

29. Charles Lutz is Director of the Office of Church and Society, American Lutheran Church. See *Lutheran Standard,* October 4, 1985, p. 39.

Chapter 6. Religion and the Public Schools

1. *Flory* v. *Sioux Falls School District,* 449 U.S. 987; and the summary of it in Baptist Joint Committee on Public Affairs, *Report from the Capitol,* November/December 1985, p. 7.

2. A helpful, if not fully balanced, summary is in John H. Bunzel, ed., *Challenge to America Schools: The Case for Standards and Values* (New York: Oxford University Press, 1983); see "Values, Resources, and Politics in America's Schools," *Daedalus,* Fall 1984; a pungent right-wing summary is John Eidsmoe, *God and Caesar: Christian Faith and Political Action* (Westchester, Ill.: Crossway, 1984), pp. 140–59; see also William Honig, *Last Chance for Our Children* (Reading, Mass.: Addison-Wesley, 1985).

3. Steven V. Monsma, "Windows and Doors in the Wall of Separation," *Christianity Today,* April 19, 1985, p. 15.

4. Martin E. Marty, *Christian Century,* November 27, 1985, p. 1103; Leo Pfeffer, *Religion, State and the Burger Court* (Buffalo: Prometheus Books, 1984), Chap. 3; this policy was reaffirmed in the 1984–85 term of the Court; *New York Times,* July 10, 1985, p. 12.

5. Erling Jorstad, *The Politics of Doomsday: Fundamentalists of the Far Right* (Nashville: Abingdon, 1970), p. 7; George Johnson, *Architects of Fear: Conspiracy Theories and Paranoia in American Politics* (Los Angeles: Jeremy P. Tarcher, 1983).

6. Tim LaHaye, *The Battle for the Mind* (Old Tappan, N.J.: Fleming H. Revell, 1980), pp. 9–19, 145; Johnson, *Architects of Fear,* pp. 172–73; Carol Flake, *Redemptorama: Culture, Politics and the New Evangelicalism* (Garden City: Doubleday, 1984), pp. 38–39; Donald Heinz, "The Struggle to Define America," as cited by Robert C. Liebman and Robert Wuthnow, eds., *The*

New Christian Right: Mobilization and Legitimation (New York: Aldine Publishing Co., 1983), pp. 133-34; *New York Times,* editorial, May 19, 1984; *Boston Globe,* editorial, May 26, 1984; these and the other newspaper accounts cited below in notes 7, 8, and 9 are drawn from the unedited, photostated reproductions of these newspaper items presented in People for the American Way, ed., *Quarterly News Clips,* April—September 1985, PAW, 1424 16th Street, N.W., Suite 601, Washington, D.C. 20036.

7. *New York Times,* February 22, 1985, p. 12; ibid., April 16, 1985.

8. *New York Times,* May 19, 1985; ibid., February 22, 1985.

9. Ibid., May 19, 1985; *Houston Post,* May 29, 1985; editorial, *New York Times,* August 20, 1985; *Wall Street Journal,* August 8, 1985.

10. Phillip E. Hammond, "The Courts and Secular Humanism," *Society,* May/June, 1984, p. 16.

11. *Time,* March 9, 1984, p. 12; "Pat Boone's 1984 School Prayer Crusade in Washington," p. 3; Donald Heinz, "The Struggle to Define America," pp. 139–42.

12. John W. Baker, "Views of the Wall," *Report from the Capitol,* May 1984, p. 10. See the statement by the American Lutheran Church, "Public Schools and Religious Practices," 1971.

13. News story, *Christianity Today,* November 22, 1985, pp. 56–57; Baptist Joint Committee, *Report* November/December 1985, p. 10.

14. James E. Wood Jr., "Religion and Education in American Church-State Relations," Wood, ed., *Religion, the State and Education* (Waco: Baylor University Press, 1984), p. 37.

15. Willard B. Gatewood Jr., "From Scopes to Creation Science: The Decline and Revival of the Evolution Controversy," *South Atlantic Quarterly,* vol. 83 (Autumn

1984), pp. 363–83; Wood, editorial in *Journal of Church and State,* vol. 24 (Spring 1982), pp. 231–34.

16. See Edward J. Larson, *Trial and Error: The American Controversy over Creation and Evolution* (New York: Oxford University Press, 1985); see Roland Mushat Frye, ed., *Is God a Creationist: The Religious Case against Creation Science* (New York: Charles Scribner, 1983); Douglas J. Futuyma, *Science on Trial: The Case for Evolution* (New York: Pantheon, 1983).

17. Donald L. Drakeman, "Religion's Place in Public Schools," *Christian Century,* May 2, 1984, pp. 462–63; *New York Times,* December 5, 1984.

18. Ibid.

19. Marty, editorial, *Christian Century,* March 14, 1984, p. 267.

Chapter 7. Faithful to What We Believe

1. Samuel S. Hill Jr., in "The Shape and Shapes of Popular Southern Piety," as quoted in David Edwin Harrell Jr., ed., *Varieties of Southern Evangelicalism* (Macon, Ga.: Mercer University Press, 1981), p. 112.

2. Bellah, et al., *Habits of the Heart* (Berkeley: University of California Press, 1985), p. 84.

3. Mary Schultz, "The Power of a Tested Tradition," *The Lutheran,* April 17, 1985, p. 32.

4. Mark Olson, "Trumpet Calls," *The Other Side,* November 1985, p. 2.

5. *The Lutheran Standard,* October 4, 1985, p. 39.

6. *The Lutheran Standard,* August 10, 1984, p. 26.

7. "Two Kingdoms," *Word and World,* 4 (Summer 1984): 277

8. *Nationhood and the Kingdom* (Nashville: Broadman, 1977), p. 85.

9. Gregory Flannery, "Father Richard Rohr: On the Cutting Edge of Church Renewal," *U.S. Catholic,* May 1984, p. 29.

10. Bellah, *Habits of the Heart,* pp. 239-40.

11. Ibid.

12. Garvey, "Politics and Religion," *Commonweal,* November 2–16, 1984, p. 585. Emphasis mine.

13. Standing Committee for Church in Society, The American Lutheran Church, "Christians as Advocates: A Primer," July 1982, p. 2.

14. Ibid.

For Further Reading

Here are some works which amplify my discussion and point to areas for further consideration. All are in paperback editions.

Bellah, Robert N., et al. *Habits of the Heart: Individualism and Commitment in American Life*. Berkeley: University of California Press, 1985.

Enroth, Ronald M. and Melton, Gordon J. *Why Cults Succeed: Where the Church Fails*. Elgin, Ill.: Brethren Press, 1985.

Gallup, George Jr. *Religion in America, 1985*. Princeton, N.J.: Princeton Religion Research Center, 1985.

Honig, William. *Last Chance for Our Children*. Reading, Mass.: Addison-Wesley, 1985.

Monsma, Stephen V. *Pursuing Justice in a Sinful World*. Grand Rapids: Eerdmans, 1984.

Naisbitt, John. *Megatrends: Ten New Directions Transforming Our Lives*. New York: Warner Books, 1982.

Neuhaus, Richard John. *Unsecular America*. Grand Rapids: Eerdmans, 1986.

Reichley, A. James. *Religion in American Public Life*. Washington, D.C.: The Brookings Institution, 1985.

Roof, Wade Clark, ed. *Religion in America Today*. Beverly Hills: Sage Publications, 1985.

DATE DUE

DEMCO 38-297